Originally published in the Italian language in April 2012 as
Il Gioco della Pizza,
© 2012 RCS Libri S.p.A., Milano.

For RCS Libri:
Editor-in-chief: Elisia Menduni
Editorial Coordinator: Paula Billingsley
Designer: TheWorldofDOT
Compositor: Paola Polastri
Photographer: Elisia Menduni
Food Stylist: Emanuela Rota
Assistant: Terese Hansén

The publishers are particularly grateful to Adelaide and all of the
Martinelli family for their kind welcome and collaboration.
Thanks to Katie Parla and Chiara Scandone for their help with
the English-language edition.

First published in the United States of America in 2013
by Rizzoli International Publications, Inc.
300 Park Avenue South
New York, NY 10010
www.rizzoliusa.com

English translation © 2013 Rizzoli International Publications, Inc.

For Rizzoli International Publications:
Translator: Natalie Danford
Editor: Christopher Steighner
Copy Editor: Leda Scheintaub
Designer: LeAnna Weller Smith

2013 2014 2015 2016 / 10 9 8 7 6 5 4 3 2 1

Distributed in the U.S. trade by Random House, New York
Printed in China
ISBN-13: 978-0-8478-4068-7
Library of Congress Catalog Control Number: 2013934389

PIZZA

GABRIELE BONCI

"The Michelangelo of dough" —VOGUE

SEASONAL RECIPES FROM ROME'S LEGENDARY PIZZARIUM

with Elisia Menduni

RIZZOLI
NEW YORK

New York · Paris · London · Milan

Contents

Foreword

Gabriele Bonci is a pure soul whose vocation is the creation of basic, even primordial food. He stands on the side of quality and naturalness. He also has boundless energy and sharply focused creativity.

Gabriele Bonci is a wonderful cook, but more than that, he's a good man. As a result he surrounds himself with good things and high-quality products. The logo that appears below was designed for him after a great deal of thought and reflection and depicts a big, kind flour creature, a gentle giant with strong hands for kneading and strong arms for hugging.

Before I got to know Gabriele, I imagined him toiling away in a huge laboratory, with an army of staff. His store, I surmised, must be an imposing temple of gastronomy. So four years ago when I first walked into his pizzeria, I was slightly disappointed. The place is about 375 square feet, or 35 square meters, total. Surely this small and chaotic space could not, as a Roman friend had informed me, be turning out the city's best pizza.

But with my first bite, as the outside of the crust shattered loudly and I began to chew the creamy interior and the crunchy interior of the crust, and as it mingled with the flavors of sweet tomato sauce and intense oregano, I understood that this was more than mere pizza. The "pizza" I had eaten up until that moment was a surrogate, a substitute, but not the real thing.

Bonci's crust is rough and a slightly drab color. It's a little acidic—not too much, but noticeably so. It's crunchy on the outside, almost crispy, and the crumb is soft and springy.

The dough for that crust is constantly evolving, but it's the toppings that change drastically from day to day and week to week. Those toppings are seasonal and often surprising. The play on contrasts is extreme, and the numerous possible options depend on creative impulse and whim. They also change depending on what suppliers have to offer. The customers who crowd into the pizzeria at all hours make their own contribution. Together they form a kind of human laboratory for testing various types of pizza, and independently, each has his or her unique taste. They constantly monitor the work as it is performed.

In eight years of research, Gabriele has created thousands of pizzas. In more than one year working on this book, I've counted (and, I confess, tasted) more than 1,500 variations, one of the most satisfying gourmet experiences of my life. What I'm left with, since I've already digested those many pizzas, is the precious gift of having a chance to work with a true artist, someone as irrational as he is absolute, and, above all, having gained a precious friend.

Elisia Menduni

BONCi

11

Destiny

I asked Lorenzo, my most passionate client, to describe the taste of my pizza. He's young and smart, and we've known each other for a few years. Lorenzo has a pure palate and a brilliant mind. I think a large part of my success is due to customers like him, with hungry minds and hungry mouths, as intelligent as they are voracious. I want to give those people a voice.

Clean intoxicating scents, brand-new textures, and dripping with pleasure. With just one bite of this version of Italy's best-known food, a symphony of enjoyment begins to play.

I remember it as if it were yesterday, but it was three years ago that I ate my first piece of pizza at Gabriele Bonci's Pizzarium in Rome. It was pizza with zucchini blossoms and anchovies.

I couldn't believe what I was tasting. What made it so unique and special was that the moment I took my first bite, I became interested in learning how it was made. A few months later, when I was lucky enough to get to know Gabriele, I began to understand what had gone into that pizza.

As Gabriele spoke about natural yeast, flour, dough, we hung on his every word. Words that I had heard a million times suddenly took on subtle and multifaceted meanings.

I'll never forget the adrenaline rush I felt that day. Gabriele was able to convey a love for what can only be described as a living food—a food that just like us humans is influenced by the weather or the circumstances of a specific day. In Gabriele's hands, pizza became something completely new—it became a vehicle for the art of cooking, creative expression, and above all a natural and healthy food accessible to all.

What really made the difference, the one thing that made this dough unique and precious, was Gabriele's extremely pure love of food and his openness in sharing his story and his thoughts with others. Gabriele's food is as unpretentious and direct as the man himself—genuine and open.

Over the years, Gabriele's gastronomic credo grew and expanded like rising dough. It led him to new baking experiences and opened new horizons as he researched techniques, time frames, and raw materials.

But the best thing of all for someone like me who has had the good luck to meet Gabriele in person is his continued desire to improve while having fun. His eyes shine like a child's when he watches people enjoy the good food that he has so carefully crafted and created.

And this craftsman has developed a new form of gastronomy that is completely outside the box. It's so revolutionary that it cannot be labeled or categorized. This new kind of humble pizza touches everyone who loves one of the most universal acts engaged in by all of humanity: eating.

Lorenzo Sandano

Gabriele Bonci: Who I Am

My mother, Severina, was the daughter of farmers. Her father left the Veneto region to farm in the Agro Pontino area in the 1950s. I'm convinced that the close connection I feel to the land was inherited from my grandfather, who was a great farmer.

The family of my father, Sergio, hailed from the Marche region. My grandmother ran a rustic trattoria in rural Cupramontana. My first ideas about food and my initial curiosity about the world of cooking can be traced to my memories of the rich lasagna known as *vincisgrassi* native to the Marche, the smell of my aunt Elda cooking meat for *bollito misto,* my uncle Fabio's dishes, and the strong cooking tradition that has been handed down through the generations in my family.

When I was little, I wanted to be a farmer like my grandfather. Then, when I was nine, I had an experience that convinced me to become a cook instead. It was the evening before Easter Sunday and we were all going out to mass together. Before my mother locked up the house, she set the dough for the special cheese pizza traditionally made for Easter under the radiator and covered the pans with a heavy cloth. When we returned, I raced to the radiator, lifted the edge of the cloth, and there I witnessed what seemed nothing short of a miracle:

At three years old on the beach at Ostia.

On the day of my First Communion.

This is me, seventeen, with my mother, Severina, in our kingdom, the kitchen.

My mother's dough had doubled in volume and was still growing. I stayed up the whole night, keeping watch over it. I thought I'd discovered a magic spell. I would love making pizza and cooking and baking in general for the rest of my life. I pinpoint that as the exact moment when my desire to become a cook was born.

Later, I went against my family's wishes and enrolled in cooking school. I had to wake up very early because it took me almost an hour to get there. The classes were on the traditional (sometimes boring) rules of cooking and working in a restaurant. One professor in particular, Antonio Ranallo, won me over with his class on the building blocks of classic cooking: stock, béchamel, risotto, mirepoix. That class helped me understand what it would mean to be a cook: the hard work, the exhaustion, the sacrifice, and the passion. Thinking about those days puts a smile on my face, and I certainly owe some of my early culinary inspiration to Antonio.

At the age of sixteen, while working in a trattoria in Abruzzo, I managed to buy myself a motor scooter. When my shift at the restaurant ended, I enjoyed driving around to various bakeries in Rome, following the enticing smell of baking bread. I was already leaning toward baking, at least subconsciously.

Often I skipped school and crisscrossed Rome in search of good things to eat. I visited most of the rotisseries and pizzerias in the city. Then one day I walked into the legendary store La Tradizione. I can still remember everything I ate that day. Renzo, one of the two owners, "baptized" me with great Italian and French cheeses and some incredible bottles of wine. It's no accident that more than ten years after that

chance visit I decided to open my own pizzeria just two hundred yards from the store.

When I was eighteen, I went to London for four months to work in a fine Italian restaurant in Wimbledon called San Lorenzo. But I wasn't very interested in the restaurant's Italian food. Instead, I was fascinated by the city's street food, most of it ethnic. I loved the Peking duck I could nibble while I walked and the enormous kebabs for sale.

When I returned to Rome, I began to train as a chef at Convivio, a restaurant with two Michelin stars. When that apprenticeship ended, I needed to earn some money, so in the afternoons after school I began working as a pastry chef for several different restaurants. But on Saturdays and Sundays I continued to visit various bakeries, and I was always interested in learning to bake bread. When I graduated from cooking school, I was hired as the chef at Simposio in the Enoteca Costantini in Piazza Cavour with Chef Arcangelo Dandini. I grew increasingly determined to set out on my own, and

in 2003 I was ready. I didn't have enough money to open a restaurant, so I decided (reluctantly at first) to open a pizzeria, selling pizza by the slice, not far from the Vatican. After a few months, I knew I'd made the right choice. I realized that I could continue to try to do my absolute best while baking pizza. I didn't have to give up my dedication to quality or my experiments.

In the early months of my new adventure, as I kneaded water and flour every day, something strange happened to me: I felt like all the yeast in the pans of dough left to rise the night before Easter had come back and was nipping at me as it fermented. I understood then that I had actually decided to become a baker, not a cook.

Since 2003 I have journeyed through the magical world of bread with my teacher, Franco Palermo, the grandfather of Roman baking. Even though I pay him a salary these days, I still feel like his apprentice, and I never stop learning from him.

A few years ago I began to make television appearances. Thanks to Antonella Clerici, Anna Moroni, and the entire staff of the show *Prova del Cuoco,* I discovered that I like communicating to a large audience. I like the idea of explaining to a lot of people at once how to make bread and pizza and how to create and nourish a starter. I love being in front of the camera.

I've grown a lot in the eight years that I've been working for myself. My work has evolved, and every day is enjoyable. I'm so grateful to my parents and especially to my wife, Elisa, who supported and encouraged me from the start and has never stopped.

Here I'm putting the finishing touches on a dish at Simposio.

Pizza the Natural Way

Eating is an ethical, important, and decisive act. Before I explain to you how to make a good pizza, I'd like to ask you to reflect on the importance of choosing to make natural pizza rather than just any old kind.

Kneading flour and water together sets off a life cycle. There is birth, growth, regeneration, and a transition to the next generation. But if you choose flour that isn't organic and high quality, there's no guarantee that you'll end up with a natural, digestible pizza. The aim is to create a pizza that doesn't leave diners feeling uncomfortably full, but instead is light and, most important, healthful.

Giving food to other people is a fundamental act of responsibility. Because I see it that way, I have never considered that responsibility to be less important than or secondary to business and turning a profit. Nourishing my pizzeria's customers as best as possible, helping them experience intense flavors without overdoing things, and offering them healthful and organic meals has always been a point of honor and a focus for me.

Following a recipe and preparing food for yourself and others must start with seeking out high-quality raw materials. Don't worry—they won't necessarily be expensive. You do need to take an active role, however, and examine your options. In other words, you can't just go to the supermarket, buy the first bag of flour you see, drop any ingredients you like onto the dough, and stick your pizza in the oven. Procuring natural, high-quality ingredients is as much a part of making the pizzas in this book as kneading the dough or baking them. Be prepared to dedicate an appropriate amount of effort and attention to locating your ingredients.

So, start by locating natural ingredients. Get into the habit of visiting farmers' markets and smaller shops; steer clear of large grocery stores. Small local producers in your area will provide good-quality products, with the added bonus that you'll enjoy direct relationships with them, which means they'll share information and professional knowledge with you. I know it's not easy. We all have busy lives and work too much and time is tight. But your health and the health of your loved ones is worth the effort.

With the entire Marino family. Grandfather Felice is standing to my left.

Caption contest: Come up with a caption for this photo.

With Roberto Liberati.

Singular Ingredients

I don't use "products" in or on my pizzas. Instead, I make my pizzas using ingredients with a history, with faces, hands, and craftsmanship behind them. It's taken me many years to find the ingredients I use, and I'm always looking for new ones.

One day, a young woman came to Pizzarium with a bouquet of Sicilian oregano. The smell was insanely good. We got to know each other, and the following summer I bought her entire oregano harvest.

My relationship with the Marino family, whose members have supplied me with flour for years, is one of the pillars on which my work stands. I have such a close relationship with them that it goes far beyond work at this point. When Grandfather Felice, a partisan in Langa during the war, bought a small mill with a natural grindstone in 1955, the entire family got involved in milling organic flour. The ancient art of grinding with round millstones is handed down from father to son, and the quality of their flour is extremely high. The process for stone-grinding flour differs depending on the grain being used. This ensures that none of the grains get "burned" and that the germ isn't damaged.

I work with Fulvio and Fausto, the latest members of the family to work at the mill, to design special flours. Together we seek out small farmers who grow less common grains and native varieties using techniques that respect the environment.

Another important partner of mine is Roberto Liberati, who owns a meat boutique in Rome. I call it a "meat boutique" rather than a "butcher shop," because Roberto isn't exactly a butcher, or rather, he's so much more than just a butcher. He personally selects all the meat sold in his family's shop in the Tuscolano neighborhood. He monitors what the animals are fed and makes sure they eat properly, are free to move about, and are raised with compassion and care. He works directly with farmers and often provides input about butchering and aging. He supplies the meat that goes into my meatballs and the prosciutto and other preserved meats that I slice and scatter on my pizzas, as well as tripe, tongue, and numerous cuts of beef.

A few years ago I got acquainted with Monica Maggio and her company, Feudo, in Zocca, which isn't far from Modena. In addition to growing incredible fruit on her eighteen hectares (about forty-five acres) of land, Monica raises heirloom-breed ducks, lambs, rabbits, geese, pheasants, and chickens. I also look for products in and around Rome. There are two people in particular who are key to my pizza. The first is Renzo Fantucci of La Tradizione, a historic gourmet store that has always educated me and sells cheese and meats from small Italian producers. This shop has a large selection and always offers products at their optimal age or level of seasoning. The second is Vincenzo Mancino, owner of DOL, which stands for Di Origine Laziale, or "of Lazio origin," a place where strictly regional products are sold. From Vincenzo I get oil, cheeses, and meats.

Look around your own area for producers and craftspeople who make their own excellent items. The time you spend seeking them out and getting to know them will never be wasted.

Pizza
School

INGREDIENTS

Flour

I make natural pizza with freshly milled flour that has plenty of germ, appropriate protein content, and the proper amount of gluten.

Let's talk about wheat. Most of the bread, focaccia, and pizza that we eat is made with wheat flour. After all, wheat is one of the most common grains on the planet. Wheat owes its prevalence over corn, rice, and rye to the fact that wheat flour is so well suited to bread baking.

The wheatberry (*Triticum*) is composed of three parts: the germ, the endosperm, and the bran. The bran (12% of the total weight) is the outer layer that holds the whole grain together. It is rich in insoluble vitamins and fiber. The endosperm (85%) is the largest portion of the grain, and it is rich in starch and protein and key to the transformation of gluten. The germ (3%) is the embryo inside the grain, and in the right conditions it turns into a new plant. It is the nutritious core of the wheatberry— rich in vitamins, fats, and minerals.

Flour is made by grinding (milling) wheatberries. The grain is gradually shelled and broken down into progressively smaller pieces, which are then sifted to a certain level of fineness depending on the kind of flour to be made. Industrial flour milling tends to completely eliminate the bran and separate out the germ from the wheat. All of the naturally occurring fat is removed, giving the resulting flour a much longer shelf life.

Whole-grain flour, made by milling the entire grain, contains more of the natural oils from the germ and the bran and for that reason it has a shorter shelf life. White flour, on the other hand, is all endosperm. The endosperm is the part of the grain with the most sugar and protein, or gluten, but it contains little fat, oil, vitamins, or minerals—the things that make wheat a complete food. For that reason, sifted white flour will last longer.

A flour's strength is indicated by its percentage of protein. A high percentage indicates that the flour contains a great deal of gluten and therefore can absorb a lot of water and create a resistant and tenacious dough that will rise slowly.

A flour with a high percentage of protein will create a dense and strong gluten web and a dough that rises slowly. A low-protein or weak flour needs very little water to form a dough or batter and rises quickly. Usually weak flours are used to make cakes and cookies, and they may also be used as a coating on fried foods or to thicken sauces. In the United States, all-purpose flour is 10 to 12% protein, and bread flour is 12 to 14% protein. For pizza, it's best to use a higher protein flour. For more information about flour and the differences between Italian flour and the flour sold in the United States, see page 252.

Flours that are labeled the same way can vary in strength depending on the brand, the time of year, and other factors.

These days, many flour manufacturers focus more on the "extraction capacity" of a variety of wheat than on its quality and strength. Nutritional elements are added and removed depending on the ultimate goal. The process of making this flour calls for extracting the germ, adding or eliminating protein, and adding or removing fiber. Often these parts are toasted and stabilized, meaning they are cooked and rendered lifeless. For example, toasted germ and bran may be mixed back into the flour.

As flour is refined, it loses a lot of what is good about it. Most of this is due to the speed of the production cycle—large-scale production is fast, and very high temperatures are reached. High heat essentially kills all the grain's nutritious elements. Industrial mills use metal cylinders that may perform anywhere from six to thirty-six rotations to make flour. As this machinery works at high speeds, it harshly manipulates the grains. The bran and germ are expelled as early as the first round of the cycle.

Natural stone grinding mills, however, work much more slowly. The grain is ground in a single cycle, so it doesn't overheat, and none of its parts (germ and bran) are removed. Thanks to this more gentle and nonviolent action on the part of the stone, the grains are broken down cylindrically and the germ remains alive inside them. It is not removed and it mixes into the flour, providing its rich and precious oil.

Natural millstones are also made using quarried natural stone that's very hard and durable. Natural stone has to be refaced occasionally—this is done by hammering it manually. That hammering

creates the correct amount of roughness on the surface of the stone. The resulting flour has the ideal characteristics for many uses—optimal starch, water absorption, and so on. Artificial millstones, on the other hand, are not hammered and are simply manufactured out of various materials.

One last thing you should know about industrial flour: the meaning of "extraction." When whole grains are ground, the resulting whole-wheat flour has a 100% extraction rate. Commonly available flours instead have an extraction rate that ranges from 65% to 85%. Flours with a higher extraction rate have more vitamins and minerals. Flour sold in a mainstream supermarket has had some of the nutritious parts—the germ and the bran—removed during processing and is therefore no longer a living flour. Usually, in order to bring it back to life, toasted bran and germ are added back in, but that's rarely enough to bring the flour back into balance. Also, it's not only unnatural but just plain silly to take the fiber out of the flour and then artificially put it back in. I can never get over that idea.

I don't use industrially made flours, and I'd like to ask you to think long and hard about using them yourself. I use only organic stone-ground flour. That flour is delivered to my pizzeria on a weekly basis, at just the right level of ripeness and freshness. It is a living thing. To be great, bread and pizza must be made with fresh ingredients. You may not have given much thought before this to flour's being fresh or stale, but flour is the main ingredient in any pizza, so it needs to be excellent.

The grooves in a hand-carved millstone keep the flour from heating up too much.

Types of Flour

The flour available in Italian supermarkets is graded on a numbering system. For example, 00 flour is a low-protein flour with a 50% extraction rate. The scale goes up from there: 0 flour has more protein and a 72% extraction rate. Flours labeled 1, 2 and whole wheat flours all have the same amount of protein, but they have increasingly high extraction rates. In the pizza I sell, I use organic farro flour with no added gluten or anything else.

Farro is an ancient grain. It was among the first types of wheat to be planted. Over time, because it was challenging to grow and had a very low yield, it was replaced with soft wheat (a descendant of *farro grande*) and hard wheat (a descendant of *farro medio,* or emmer wheat). See the discussion of flour on page 252 for more information on farro and for substitutions.

Storage

It is always best to use fresh flour, of course, but I can't expect you to get a shipment of flour every week the way I do at Pizzarium. Store any unused flour in a cool, dry place (64°F / 18°C maximum) in tightly sealed containers and far from any heat sources. If you buy 10-pound (5-kilogram) bags of flour or larger bags, you can divide them into 1-pound (500-gram) portions and keep those in the freezer for six to eight months. The ideal way to store flour is to place it in a glass jar and keep it in the refrigerator for up to one month. Whole-grain flour can go bad rather quickly, especially in the summer: Keep an eye on it.

Salt

Salt is a key ingredient. It provides flavor and color and serves to stabilize the dough, keeping it from rising too quickly. When dough is rising, the yeast cannot consume all the sugars in the flour. It is thanks to the residual sugars and the salt in the dough that pizza crust has a lovely caramelized golden color.

Salt must be added after the yeast is added, however, or it will slow down the rising process too much. This is especially true if you are using fresh cake yeast.

There are many types of salt available these days. I prefer sea salt with no additives.

Water

With the addition of water, the starches in flour swell up and the proteins are reactivated. Water is a key ingredient in pizza. I suggest using bottled flat (not sparkling) mineral water, because tap water varies greatly from place to place and it's impossible for me to know what the water is like in your particular area. If you don't want to go to the expense of purchasing bottled water, filter your tap water, or simply fill a container with water the night before you plan to make your dough and let it sit overnight. The impurities will sink to the bottom—just be sure not to move the container around too much when you're pouring it out.

Water with too much chlorine slows the rising process, and water with too much calcium and magnesium, usually termed "hard water," can toughen gluten, which will also slow the process.

The temperature of the water you use is also important. Your flour and yeast should always be

at the same room temperature when you start. Water, however, can be heated or cooled in order to manipulate the rising process—heating it will speed rising and cooling it will slow rising down.

Yeast

Yeast is a group of single-celled organisms. The best known of these is *Saccharomyces cerevisiae.* Every kind of yeast feeds on the sugars in flour in order to set off the fermentation process. During this phase, enzymes produced by the yeast transform the sugars into carbon dioxide and alcohol and make the dough rise.

There are basically three kinds of yeast that you can use:

Cake yeast

This type of yeast is sold in 20-gram cakes wrapped in foil and contains 70% water. It is not as common in the United States as it is in the rest of the world, though you will find it occasionally. It is very delicate, and though it is usually found in a store's refrigerated case, it may not have been stored at a steady temperature while it was shipped to the store, which can cause problems. I don't recommend it.

Dry yeast

Dry yeast—whether labeled active dry or instant— is sold in packets. The yeast in those packets has been "put to sleep," and wakes up upon contact with water. This type of yeast is much more stable and provides more consistent results than cake yeast. Active dry yeast needs to be combined with water before it is added to the dough, but instant yeast is simply added with the other dry ingredients. For this reason, I prefer instant.

Natural yeast

Natural yeast is made by keeping a small piece of flour-and-water dough (or a small piece of dough from a batch made with natural yeast) and allowing it to ferment. In addition to *Saccharomyces,* natural yeast contains lactic and acetic acid. Also known as a "sourdough starter" or a "mother dough," natural yeast is a living yeast. Making natural yeast and keeping it alive does take a little more effort than simply opening a package, but the payoff is bread and pizza that stay fresh longer and are easier to digest. (Cake yeast, by contrast, contains living cells that die off very quickly.) On page 67 in the chapter on basic doughs, I explain how to make and store your own natural yeast.

Olive Oil

Many different types of fats are used to make bread, including lard and butter. But for pizza, you should use only extra-virgin olive oil. The fat keeps the dough soft and flavorful. Pizza made with extra-virgin olive oil dough also lasts longer. Extra-virgin olive oil has very low acidity (1% on average), which makes it ideal. It is also drizzled on top of finished pizzas as a condiment.

TOOLS

You probably expect me to rattle off a long list of accessories and gadgets that you need to run out and purchase in order to craft perfect pizzas. Forget about it—you probably already have the very few tools you'll need.

You don't need to head to your nearest kitchen appliance store. Just take a look around your own kitchen for the pans, spatulas, bowls, and scales you need. An old wooden spoon is always better than a new one anyway, and you don't need any unusual technical tools to make great pizza. The most important tools are your own hands and the love you'll use when creating the dough.

Scale

Use a scale to measure ingredients by weight. It's important to be exact when working with a living dough, which is a variable process. The measurements are the few completely fixed points in these recipes, so you want to hit those targets.

There are excellent digital scales available for measuring both large and small quantities. Be sure that you can adjust to tare weight to account for the weight of the container (in other words, you want to be able to put a bowl on the scale and then set it to zero so that you are only weighing the flour in the bowl and not the bowl itself) and that it can hold a large bowl.

Mixer

I'm tempted to try to convince you that kneading by hand is the only way to make a dough, but I know some of you won't listen.

I have a friend who lives in Caiazzo, in the Caserta area, who has shown me many times that you can make incredible pizza dough in a *madia,* a traditional Italian bread cupboard, using only your hands. You can achieve excellent elasticity and wonderful results.

It's true that using your hands takes a little more time and effort, though. And the results you get with a mixer aren't bad—certainly commercial bakers use mixers. But another strike against the mixer is that it seems silly to get the whole mixer and the paddle and the bowl dirty when you're working with just a few cups of flour. Wouldn't you rather have your cleanup consist of washing a bowl and a wooden spoon?

If you insist on relying on technology, you will need a heavy-duty stand mixer with a 5-quart (5-liter) bowl. There are lots of different stand mixers available, and they come with various attachments: whisks, paddles, beaters, spiral hooks. Use the attachment indicated for dough, which is usually a single piece (not two beaters, for example) and specifically labeled as such. My dough is very liquid, so your mixer won't overheat or be overtaxed, which can sometimes happen with appliances designed for home use.

Cloths

You will need a few cloths. Choose linen or cotton with no dye. They should not be brand-new. Set these cloths aside and dedicate them solely to dough; do not use them for anything else. Keep them in a separate drawer and do not wash them with detergent. Use only boiling water if you do need to wash them, but you will likely be able to simply brush them off and shake them out before storing them. Over time, these cloths will become impregnated with yeast and other substances that encourage dough to rise.

Bench Scraper

A bench scraper is a wide metal blade that is used—as the name implies—to scrape the work surface and also is excellent for cutting dough into portions, as the dough won't stick to the blade.

Pans

Pans should be thin, without reinforced bottoms. Over the years I've learned that the less a pan costs, the better the pizza it will make. A standard rectangular pizza pan or half sheet pan that's about 13 inches by 18 inches will make a pizza that supplies four generous servings.

Sieve

Sieves have been around for ages. The best kind for our purposes is made of fine metal mesh attached to a wooden frame. If you use flour from a bag that has not just been opened or is not perfectly fresh, sift it to create a more homogenous dough.

Wooden Board

You need a wooden board, untreated and unfinished but perfectly flat, to use as a work surface for making your pizza. Wood is absolutely the ideal surface for this.

Oven

Every oven is different. Your first assignment is to get to know your oven. Is it convection or conventional? Gas or electric? Does it have coils? If so, where are they and what shape are they? Most important, what is the actual oven temperature?

Conventional ovens are the best choice for making pizza at home, though you do need to keep an eye on the bottom heating element, which can burn the bottom of the dough.

Electric ovens tend to cook less strongly from the bottom. It is generally best to bake pizza on the bottom shelf, set at the lowest level possible. Convection ovens tend to dry out pizza—avoid them if possible.

The dough I make isn't really ideal for cooking in a wood-burning oven, but if you are lucky enough to have access to one, you can try it. Just keep a very close watch on the pizza as it cooks. A wood-burning oven reaches temperatures of 575°F (300°C) or higher, so it will cook a pizza in just a few minutes.

A bench scraper with a metal blade is useful for portioning dough.

TECHNIQUES

We can write all we want about working with yeast and yeast-risen dough, and I've done just that in this book, but that information is always general. There's nothing set in stone or standardized about 40 percent of my process, and the same goes for you. Be flexible, improvise, and adjust. The environment, including temperature, humidity level, the presence of bacteria in the air, and even your mood and energy level, can have a big impact on the creation of even a simple pizza. Learn these techniques and try the recipes a few times, and you'll start to get a feel for them. These recipes are intended simply as useful starting points; create your own rules.

That said, you do need to understand some basic processes before you begin.

Mixing

During this part of the process, all of the ingredients are combined. I suggest you mix the dough in a large bowl with a wooden spoon or spatula, rather than using your hands and kneading it on a wooden board. If you use a bowl and a spoon you won't get dirty and, more important, you won't waste any of the dough. (When you knead, bits of dough stick to the board and to your hands. It might seem like a negligible amount of dough gets lost this way, but it does add up, and it's a shame to waste any of it.)

To start, mix the yeast with the flour (1). Then add the water (2, 3, 4). You want to add enough water so that the dough is soft and can be mixed with a spoon. Start with the amount provided in the recipe, then gradually add more if needed. Last, after everything is well mixed (5, 6) add the salt and the oil (7, 8).

If you prefer to use a stand mixer, run it on low speed in the beginning and gradually increase the speed (never taking it to maximum) only at the very end.

What's going on while you're doing this? Thanks to proteins (gliadin and glutenin) in flour, when flour enters into contact with water it "comes to life," and the transformation of gluten is set off. Basically, when flour and water meet, a process begins that results in the formation of an elastic weblike structure that can trap the starch and gas produced naturally as dough rises.

You can tell how elastic the gluten in your dough is by pinching off a small piece and conducting this test: Rinse the little ball of dough briefly in water, then begin to stretch the dough, pulling it as long as possible (9). If the dough forms a very thin and almost transparent sheet, the gluten has developed fully and the dough is ready for its first rising.

First Rising

At this point, the dough will be very soft and shaggy (1). Don't worry about any lumps; as it ferments, it will become more consistent. Generously oil a large clean bowl and place the dough in it (you can use the same bowl you used for mixing, but rinse it out first), then set the dough aside to rest for at least 1 hour in a draft-free corner, covered with a heavy cloth (a piece of canvas is ideal) at room temperature (2).

After the stress of the previous phase, the dough has to rest. As it rises, the starches from the flour transform into sugars. This is due to amylase, an enzyme in flour that changes starch into maltose when it gets wet. Next, yeast feeds on the sugar, producing alcohol and carbon dioxide. After the first round of fermentation, sometimes called the first rise, the dough is smooth (3).

Folding

Once the first rising is finished, the dough is folded at regular intervals in order to incorporate more air into it.

Generously flour the wooden board you are using as a work surface. Overturn the bowl where the dough was rising and let the dough drop to the surface (1, 2). Press very gently with your fingertips to make it a rough rectangle. Try not to deflate the dough too much (3). Pull the lower end of the rectangle toward you, stretching the dough, and bring the edge up to the middle of the rectangle to make a pocket in the dough (4). Do the same with the top end, pulling it gently toward the bottom and sealing it to the dough (5).

Turn the dough 90 degrees so that the seam is now perpendicular to you (6). Again flatten the dough a little and then fold it again: Bring the top edge to the middle and seal, then bring the bottom edge to the middle and seal. Rotate the dough 90 degrees. Repeat this at least three times total and let the dough rest with the seam side on the bottom. The dough should be puffy from the air that's been introduced and the surface should be smooth and drier than it was previously (7, 8).

Repeat this process three times in 1 hour, waiting 15 to 20 minutes in between each series of folds. Folding the dough this way eliminates some of the carbon dioxide produced during the first rising, making room for more air to be incorporated during the second round of rising, which is slower. Additionally, the gluten threads are pulled, strengthened, and realigned, and the internal temperature of the dough becomes consistent (9–20).

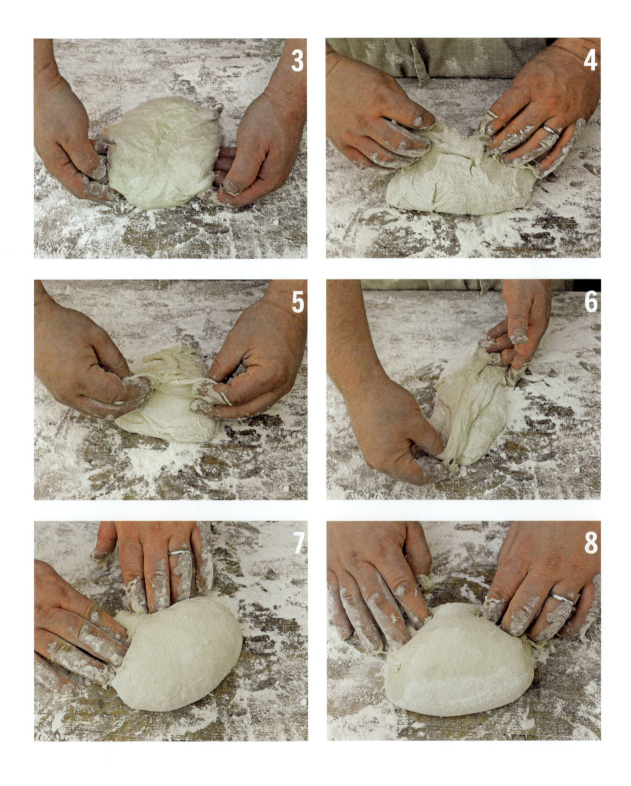

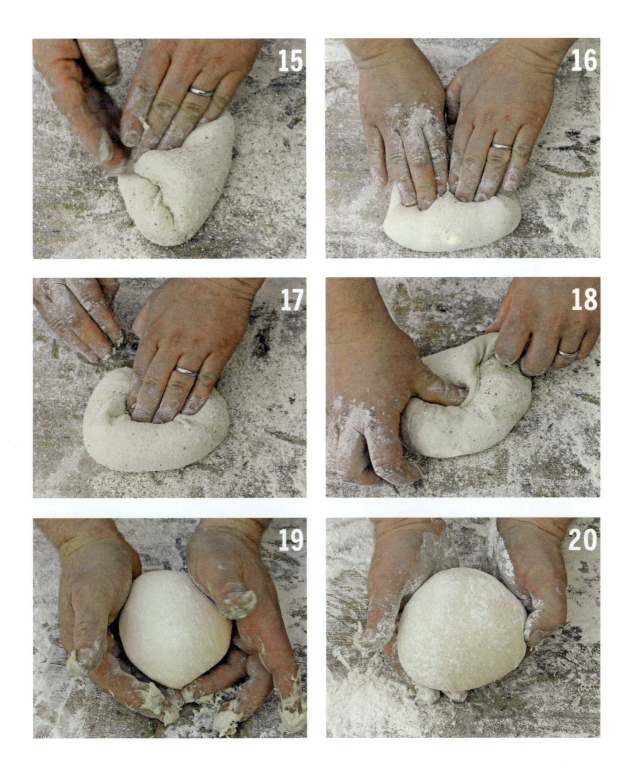

Second Rising

Once the dough has undergone the folding process, it should be puffy and smooth. Generously oil a bowl (again, you can use the same bowl you used previously, but wash it and dry it) that is at least twice as big as the volume of the dough (1). Place your dough in the center of the bowl, smooth side up.

Drizzle a little oil on the top of the dough and rub it over the surface, then cover the bowl with plastic wrap or a flat-weave dish towel (2) and place it in the refrigerator (preferably on the lowest shelf) for 18 to 24 hours. Photo (3) below shows the dough before and after the second rising.

Dividing the Dough

Remove the dough from the refrigerator and let it sit for at least 10 minutes so that it is not quite so chilly. The dough will have increased noticeably in volume. Decide how much dough you want to use. Generally, 12 ounces (350 grams) of dough is the perfect amount for a medium-size pizza.

Turn the dough out of the bowl and onto a floured work surface. At this point, you want to manipulate the dough as little as possible and you don't want to pull on it or tear it. Use a bench scraper or sharp knife to cut it neatly (1, 2). Weigh the pieces of dough. Add or remove small amounts of dough to get the portion that you want, but try to handle the dough as little as possible. (After you've made pizza a few times, you'll develop an eye and be able to portion the dough easily.) When you have the right amount, fold the dough following the instructions on page 46 (just one cycle), then round it into a ball with the seam side underneath (3).

Let the dough rest at room temperature until it doubles in size and feels very soft and puffy, about 1½ hours.

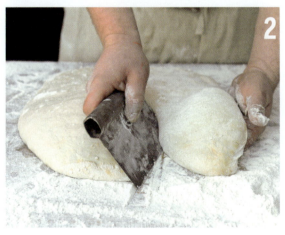

Stretching

The process of shaping the dough seems simple enough, but it's actually fairly delicate. After all, you've now been working on this dough for more than 24 hours. The last thing you want to do is to ruin all that hard work by rolling it or tearing it or bursting the bubbles that have formed.

First, oil the pan (I always like a little drizzle even if the dough won't stick without it) and set it aside.

Flour the work surface (you can toss in a handful of semolina flour if you like its texture on the bottom of your pizza) and place one ball of dough on it. Press on the dough softly with your fingertips,

roughly shaping it to fit your pan (1, 2). When the dough is a rough rectangle (3), turn it so that one of the short ends is facing you (4). Rest your left hand on the far right corner of the rectangle so that your arm crosses the dough diagonally (5). Use your right hand to fold half of the dough over your left arm (6) and then move your right hand underneath the dough so that your arms are parallel with your palms down and the dough spread across your arms (7). As you perform this motion, gently stretch the dough. Set the stretched dough on the oiled pan (8).

Cooking

Your oven should be very hot. It is a good idea to invest in an oven thermometer so you can calibrate your oven to the proper temperature; most home ovens are not perfectly accurate. The oven should be preheated to the temperature indicated in the recipe, which will be from 450°F to 475°F (220°C to 250°C). Start at the higher temperature and decrease gradually if you aren't satisfied with the results. During baking, most of the water in the dough evaporates, the starches solidify, sugars caramelize, and a crust forms on the surface.

BASIC DOUGHS

There are three basic doughs that you can use to make the pizzas in this book. In the pizzeria, I use the third one (Whole Grain Pizza Dough, page 64) exclusively, but my situation is a little different from yours, because I prepare hundreds of pounds of pizza dough every day.

The three doughs I'm including here are the ones I make at home and in the pizza and bread-baking classes that I teach frequently in Italy. They use different ingredients and different types of yeast, but they're all fairly easy to make and should give you excellent results every time.

Three Types of Dough

Each of the pizza recipes in this book suggests one of these three doughs, but you can use any of the three to match your personal taste and what you intend to do with the pizza, and which types of flour you have on hand. Really, any of these three doughs will work with any of the recipes in the book. Just remember that for all of them you need to follow the steps laid out in the Techniques chapter on pages 40 to 54: mixing, first rising, folding, second rising, dividing the dough, stretching, and baking. See page 252 for more information on the types of flour used and U.S. equivalents for Italian flour.

White

- 2½ teaspoons (7 grams) instant yeast
- 8 cups (1 kilogram) bread flour
- 3 cups (700 grams) room temperature tap or bottled water
- 1 tablespoon plus 1 teaspoon (20 grams) fine sea salt
- 3 tablespoons (40 grams) olive oil

Mixed Grain

- 4 cups (500 grams) Buratto flour (see page 252)

- 2 cups (250 grams) light spelt flour

- 2 cups (250 grams) whole-grain farro or spelt flour

- 3 cups (700 grams) room temperature water

- 3 tablespoons (40 grams) olive oil

- 1 tablespoon plus 1 teaspoon (20 grams) fine sea salt

- 1½ teaspoons (4 grams) instant yeast or ½ cup (100 grams) natural yeast (page 67)

Whole Grain

- 4 cups (500 grams) Buratto flour (see page 252)
- 4 cups (500 grams) whole-grain farro or spelt flour
- 3⅓ cups (800 grams) room temperature tap or bottled water
- 3 tablespoons (40 grams) olive oil
- 1 tablespoon plus 1 teaspoon (20 grams) fine sea salt
- 5½ ounces/¾ cup (150 grams) natural yeast (page 67)

Natural Yeast

I'm all for natural ingredients, but these days I think people are positively obsessed with natural yeast. Natural yeast definitely yields different results than commercial yeast. Dough that rises using the yeasts that are naturally present in the air is easier to digest and better for you. Developing your own yeast is definitely worth a try. After all, there was a time when industrial yeast was not yet available, so all bread and pizza was made without it. But if your efforts don't produce a useful starter, or if you don't have time to make one, or if you just want the reliability of standardized, store-bought yeast, there's really nothing wrong with it. Actually, I think it's one of the best food products invented in the last hundred years.

Liquid Starter

Natural yeast is created by letting water and flour go sour. Various microorganisms that are already present in flour, water, and the surrounding environment develop in this primordial mixture.

The first thing that you have to do is to try to lure them into your trap. The best type of flour for this is natural rye flour, which has the highest sugar content of any flour. Mix 3 tablespoons of rye flour with enough room temperature water to make a mixture with the consistency of sour cream and place the mixture in a glass jar. Place a piece of cheesecloth over the top, secure it with a rubber band, and wait 48 hours. After 48 hours, add a little more rye flour and a little water, cover with the cheesecloth again, and wait another 48 hours. Repeat this for 10 days. Eventually, the mixture will begin to expand. When the 10 days are up, the mixture should still be fairly liquid and it should be bubbling energetically.

Liquid starter needs to be refreshed, because the microorganisms need to feed on something. When your starter seems nice and mature, you can refresh it every 48 hours if you keep it at room temperature and every 4 to 5 days if you keep it in the refrigerator. To refresh this type of starter, knead together equal parts (by weight) active starter, flour, and water. Keep the refreshed starter at room temperature until you're ready to use it.

Firm Starter

You can also store your starter in the form of a firm dough. Weigh the starter (or the amount of starter you want) and add 50 percent of its weight in flour. Mix until well combined; you will have a rather stiff ball of dough. Place it in a small bowl, cover with a dish towel, and put a rubber band around the dish towel. Refresh every 48 hours at the most. To refresh a firm starter, take out a piece of the starter, weigh it, and add an equal amount of flour in weight and 50 percent water in weight.

starter on the first day

fourth day

sixth day

tenth day

Activators

The method on page 67 is the easiest way to create a starter, but you can also add other foods to "activate" your starter—these include honey, vinegar, yogurt, fruit juice (apple juice is best), tomato juice, mashed grapes, and other substances that naturally contain sugar. You can even use yogurt from the very beginning, refreshing the starter every 48 hours for at least 1 week. Yogurt ensures fermentation, as it is already fermented, so you can be certain your starter will work. (The starter will have a different flavor, which some people prefer.)

If you want to make a yogurt starter, use:
- ¼ cup (60 grams) plain organic yogurt
- ¾ cup (100 grams) bread flour
- ½ cup (100 grams) water

Mix everything together and let ferment for 1 week, adding water and flour every 48 hours. When the yeast has become active, after about 7 days, proceed as above, refreshing the starter every 2 days with equal amounts (by weight) starter, flour, and water.

Before Using

Once your starter, no matter which type, is active, always refresh it before using. In this book, when I call for natural yeast, I'm referring to a refreshed portion of any of these types of starters.

To prepare a starter for use, 1 to 2 hours before you plan to make the dough, remove 3½ ounces/½ cup (100 grams) of starter from the jar and combine it with 3½ ounces/¾ cup (100 grams) flour. Use the same kind of flour that you will be using for the dough as a whole.

Once the flour has been added to the starter, add the equal amount (by weight) in water (about ½ cup in this case). (The easiest way to do this is to place a small bowl on your scale, zero out the scale, and then add 3½ ounces/100 grams each of starter, flour, and water.) Beat with a wooden spoon until smooth, cover, and set aside at room temperature for 1 to 2 hours. The starter should be active and bubbly, and you can then proceed with the dough recipe.

Fermentation

Yeast causes fermentation. The word "fermentation" derives from the Latin word *fervere,* or "return to a boil." Indeed, when a dough begins to rise, a chemical transformation occurs and bubbles form.

Dry yeast sets off alcoholic fermentation that produces alcohol and carbon dioxide. But fermentation using a natural starter occurs through a dynamic balance of different types of yeasts: various strains of *Saccharomyces* and lactic acid bacteria of the *Lactobacillus* type.

Sourdough fermentation is therefore lactic and not simply alcoholic. In addition to alcohol and carbon dioxide, lactic acid and acetic acid are produced. The dough's acidic environment protects the sourdough from contamination by other types of bacteria, and it grows stronger as time passes.

The advantage of lactic fermentation over alcoholic fermentation is proteolysis, the first breakdown of gluten proteins set off by lactic bacteria. That breakdown is much stronger than the breakdown that occurs with alcoholic fermentation. Bread and other items made from dough that rises with a natural starter is thus easier to digest. Thanks to the proteolytic enzyme of the lactic bacteria, a naturally risen dough is actually "predigested" and easier for our bodies to process.

Some Useful Advice

If after 48 hours your starter appears to be inert, refresh it and wait another 48 hours. If it still does not look active, throw it out and start over.

The best way to store starter is to keep it on the bottom shelf of your refrigerator, where the temperature remains most stable. Keep it in a glass container; plastic really isn't suited to storing starters. A starter prepared as described on pages 67 and 70 and properly refreshed regularly should last for years, or even indefinitely.

Pizza Recipes

YEAR-ROUND
PIZZAS

Tomato Pizza

- 1 (12-ounce /350-gram) ball White Pizza Dough (page 60)
- Extra-virgin olive oil to taste
- 2 cups (500 grams) canned peeled tomatoes, drained
- Fine sea salt to taste
- Fresh oregano leaves to taste

Preheat the oven to 450°F to 475°F (220°C to 250°C).

Stretch the dough and place it in a well-oiled pan, pressing with your fingertips, but not dimpling the entire surface. Place the tomatoes in a small bowl. Drizzle the tomatoes with a little oil, season with salt, and toss to combine. Squeeze the tomatoes through your fingers to break them up, then rub them (without pressing) all over the surface of the dough. Sprinkle with a small amount of additional salt.

Bake the pizza until golden brown and well-risen, about 25 minutes.

Remove the pizza from the oven and sprinkle the oregano leaves on top. Drizzle with a small amount of additional oil. Serve hot.

Use firm, peeled tomatoes and drain them well, keeping only the flesh.

For an especially flavorful oregano, look for Sicilian oregano picked in late summer.

Potato Pizza

- 9 ounces (250 grams) mozzarella
- 1 (12-ounce / 350-gram) ball White Pizza Dough (page 60)
- Extra-virgin olive oil to taste
- 1 pound (500 grams) yellow potatoes (see Note), such as Yukon golds, boiled, peeled, and cooled
- Fine sea salt to taste

Preheat the oven to 450°F to 475°F (220°C to 250°C).

Dice the cheese and pat it dry with paper towels. Stretch the dough and place it in a well-oiled pan. Sprinkle the cheese over the dough. Crush the potatoes through your fingers onto the dough. Drizzle with a little oil.

Bake the pizza until golden brown and well-risen, about 25 minutes.

Remove the pizza from the oven, season with salt, and serve hot.

I use Acria potatoes, which grow in Abruzzo in the Avezzano area. Yukon gold potatoes make a good substitute in the United States. I prefer yellow potato varieties for this pizza because they tend to have low water content and do a better job of absorbing the flavor of the other ingredients.

Classic Pizza with Tomato Sauce, Mozzarella, and Basil

- 1 (12-ounce / 350-gram) ball White Pizza Dough. (page 60)
- Extra-virgin olive oil to taste
- 2 cups (500 grams) canned peeled tomatoes
- Fine sea salt to taste
- 1 pound (500 grams) buffalo mozzarella
- 3 cups loosely packed (100 grams) basil leaves

Preheat the oven to 450°F to 475°F (220°C to 250°C).

Stretch the dough and place it in a well-oiled pan. Place the tomatoes in a small bowl. Drizzle the tomatoes with a little oil, season with salt, and toss to combine. Squeeze the tomatoes through your fingers to break them up, and drop them onto the dough.

Bake the pizza until golden brown and well-risen, about 25 minutes.

Remove the pizza from the oven. Immediately tear the cheese into pieces by hand and scatter it over the pizza. Scatter on the basil leaves, then drizzle with some oil and season with salt.

If you prefer a pizza with more thoroughly melted cheese, you can put the mozzarella on top before putting the pizza in the oven, but don't use buffalo mozzarella, as it will create a pool of water on top of the pizza. Imported Italian fior di latte mozzarella is the best mozzarella to melt in the oven, but it's often hard to find.

Focaccia with Cherry Tomatoes

- 1 (12-ounce / 350-gram) ball Mixed Grain Pizza Dough (page 62)
- Extra-virgin olive oil to taste
- 1 pint (300 grams) grape tomatoes, halved
- Fine sea salt to taste
- Oregano leaves to taste
- 14 ounces (400 grams) yellow onions

Place the dough in a well-oiled pan. A 14-inch circular deep-dish pizza pan would work well here. Using your fingertips, stretch the dough to fit the pan.

Toss the halved tomatoes with a generous amount of oil, salt, and oregano. Scatter the tomatoes over the dough, then press them lightly into the dough. Thinly slice the onions, rinse them in cold water, dry them with a dish towel, and scatter them over the pizza. Set the pizza aside for 1 hour at room temperature. The dough should rise further so that the tomatoes are slightly embedded in the dough.

When the dough has been rising in the pan for about 30 minutes, preheat the oven to 450°F to 475°F (220°C to 250°C).

Bake the pizza until golden brown and well-risen, about 25 minutes.

Remove the pizza from the oven and serve hot.

SUMMER PIZZAS

Zucchini Crostino

- 1 (12-ounce / 350-gram) ball White Pizza Dough (page 60)
- Extra-virgin olive oil to taste
- 10½ ounces (300 grams) mozzarella
- Freshly ground black pepper to taste
- 14 ounces (400 grams) ribbed Roman zucchini or other dry type of zucchini

At Pizzarium, we call any pizza that has a lot of mozzarella and only one other topping a crostino. *These are fairly quick to make, and the weight of the generous portion of mozzarella keeps the dough from rising particularly high, which results in a crunchy and tasty crust.*

Preheat the oven to 450°F to 475°F (220°C to 250°C).

Stretch the dough and place it in a well-oiled pan. Pull the cheese into large chunks by hand and scatter about half of it over the dough. Season with pepper.

Slice the zucchini into very thin rounds. (Use a mandoline if you have one.) Scatter the zucchini in an even layer over the cheese. Scatter the remaining cheese on top of the zucchini. Drizzle with a generous amount of oil.

Bake the pizza until golden brown and well-risen, about 25 minutes.

Remove the pizza from the oven and serve hot.

Pizza with Figs

- 1 (12-ounce / 350-gram) ball White Pizza Dough (page 60)
- Extra-virgin olive oil to taste
- 16 very ripe fresh figs (see Note)
- 1 sprig rosemary
- Fine sea salt to taste

Preheat the oven to 450°F to 475°F (220°C to 250°C).

Stretch the dough and place it in a well-oiled pan. Peel half of the figs. Break the peeled figs apart by hand and scatter them over the surface of the dough. Drizzle with a generous amount of oil.

Bake the pizza until the figs are very soft, golden, and almost caramelized, about 25 minutes.

Remove the pizza from the oven and let it cool for a few minutes so that it is no longer piping hot. Just before serving, quarter the remaining (unpeeled) figs and scatter them over the pizza. Strip the rosemary leaves from the stem and scatter them over the top. Season with salt and drizzle with a generous amount of oil.

NOTE: *Late-summer figs are best for this recipe, as they are very sweet and thin-skinned.*

Pizza with Eggplant Parmigiana

- 1 pound (500 grams) thin eggplants
- Fine sea salt to taste
- Extra-virgin olive oil to taste
- 1 (12-ounce / 350-gram) ball White Pizza Dough (page 60)
- 2 cups (500 grams) crushed tomatoes, canned or fresh
- 12 ounces (350 grams) mozzarella
- 9 ounces (250 grams) Parmigiano-Reggiano, grated
- Leaves of 1 bunch basil

Cut the eggplants lengthwise into ½-inch (1½-cm) slices. Sprinkle the eggplant slices with salt and layer them between paper towels. Set aside until they give up their liquid, about 2 hours. Rinse the eggplant slices and pat them dry thoroughly. Heat a generous amount of oil in a sauté pan and brown the eggplant, cooking it in batches if necessary to keep from crowding the pan.

Preheat the oven to 450°F to 475°F (220°C to 250°C).

Stretch the dough and place it in a well-oiled pan. Combine the crushed tomatoes with a little oil and salt and spread them over the surface of the dough. Shred the mozzarella cheese by hand and scatter it over the tomatoes. Sprinkle about three-quarters of the Parmigiano-Reggiano cheese over the mozzarella cheese.

Bake the pizza until the surface is browned and crunchy, about 25 minutes.

Remove the pizza from the oven and arrange the fried eggplant on top. Sprinkle with the remaining Parmigiano-Reggiano cheese. Scatter the basil leaves on top and serve hot.

Pizza with Prosciutto and Figs

- 2 (12-ounce / 350-gram) balls Mixed Grain Pizza Dough (page 62)
- Extra-virgin olive oil to taste
- 16 ripe fresh figs, sliced
- Thinly sliced prosciutto (see Note) to taste

Preheat the oven to 450˚F to 475˚F (220˚C to 250˚C).

Make a "double" pizza: Stretch out 1 ball of dough and place it in a well-oiled pan. Brush the top of the dough with additional oil. On a lightly floured surface, stretch out the second ball of dough and place it gently on top of the first. (Once baked, this type of pizza is easy to split and make into a sandwich. Slicing a pizza baked in one piece lengthwise way may break up the pockets in the dough, and that's a shame after you've worked so hard to help the dough rise properly.)

Bake the pizza until deep golden brown and well-risen, about 30 minutes.

Remove the pizza from the oven and pull apart the layers; they should separate easily. Make sandwiches by placing the sliced figs and prosciutto between the layers.

NOTE: *For the greatest contrast between sweet figs and savory prosciutto, look for a prosciutto that has been subject to medium- or long-term aging; prosciutto from central Italy is especially good.*

93

Pizza with Potatoes, Eggplant Puree, Buffalo Mozzarella, and Rosemary Ash

- 1 (12-ounce / 350-gram) ball White Pizza Dough (page 60)
- Extra-virgin olive oil to taste
- 10 ounces (300 grams) yellow potatoes, such as Yukon golds, boiled and peeled
- 1 pound (500 grams) eggplant
- Fine sea salt to taste
- 10 ounces (300 grams) buffalo mozzarella
- Sweet paprika to taste
- 1 sprig rosemary, rinsed and thoroughly dried
- Freshly ground black pepper to taste

Preheat the oven to 450°F to 475°F (220°C to 250°C).

Stretch out the dough and place it in a well-oiled pan. With your hands, crush the potatoes and scatter the pieces over the dough.

Bake the pizza until golden brown and well-risen, about 25 minutes.

While the pizza is baking, wrap the eggplant in aluminum foil. Place the foil-wrapped eggplant directly on top of the burner on a gas stove (if you don't have a gas stove, use a grill or broiler) and cook for 8 minutes on each side, or until the eggplant is charred and very soft. Open the foil, cut the eggplant in half, and use a spoon to scoop out the cooked eggplant pulp.

Remove the pizza from the oven and spread the eggplant over the surface. Season with salt. Tear the cheese with your hands and scatter it over the eggplant. Season with a little paprika.

Place a square of aluminum foil on the counter. Place the rosemary sprig directly over the gas burner, turning it frequently so that it doesn't burn but the leaves char. This should take about 1 minute. Remove the charred rosemary from the flame and place it on top of the foil. Some of the charred leaves should fall onto the foil. If not, shake the sprig a little. Sprinkle a bit of this rosemary ash over the pizza. (Don't overdo it or the pizza will taste too smoky.) Season with pepper and serve immediately.

Pizza with Octopus and Potatoes

- 1 fresh or frozen octopus, about 3 pounds (1½ kilograms), cleaned
- Fine sea salt to taste
- 1 rib celery
- 2 tomatoes
- 1 carrot
- 1 onion
- 1 (12-ounce / 350-gram) ball Mixed Grain Pizza Dough (page 62)
- Extra-virgin olive oil to taste
- 2 pounds (1 kilogram) yellow potatoes, such as Yukon golds, boiled and peeled
- Sweet paprika to taste
- Minced flat-leaf parsley to taste

Place the octopus in a stockpot with a generous amount of salted cold water. Add the celery, tomatoes, carrot, and onion. Bring to a boil, then turn down the heat and simmer until the octopus is tender, about 1 hour. Let the octopus cool in the pot until it reaches room temperature.

Preheat the oven to 450°F to 475°F (220°C to 250°C).

Stretch out the dough and place it in a well-oiled pan.

Bake the pizza until golden brown and well-risen, about 25 minutes.

While the pizza is baking, remove the octopus from the liquid. Dry the octopus well and char it on a griddle. If the octopus is very large, chop it into large pieces.

Remove the pizza from the oven and use a potato ricer to rice the potatoes, letting them drop onto the pizza. Place the octopus on top of the potatoes. Season with paprika, parsley, salt, and a drizzle of oil. Serve hot.

Spicy Tomato-Anchovy Pizza

- 2 cups (500 grams) canned peeled tomatoes
- Extra-virgin olive oil to taste
- Fine sea salt to taste
- Fennel seeds to taste
- 1 salted anchovy, rinsed, boned, and chopped
- 4 cloves garlic, peeled and crushed
- 1 (12-ounce / 350-gram) ball White Pizza Dough (page 60)
- 3 fresh chiles (such as peperoncini)
- Minced flat-leaf parsley to taste

Preheat the oven to 450°F to 475°F (220°C to 250°C).

Crush the tomatoes by hand. In a small bowl, toss the crushed tomatoes with a little oil, salt, fennel seeds, the anchovy, and the garlic.

Stretch out the dough and place it in a well-oiled pan. Spread the tomato mixture over the dough.

Bake the pizza until golden brown and well-risen, about 25 minutes.

While the pizza is baking, with a mortar and pestle, grind the chiles. (Seed them first if you don't want the pizza to be too spicy.) As you grind the chiles, drizzle in enough oil to make a creamy paste. Toss in the parsley and grind slightly to combine.

Remove the pizza from the oven and spoon the spicy mixture on top. Serve warm.

Pizza with Roast Pork, Tomatoes, Apricots, and Peppers

- 1 (1-pound / 500-gram) pork roast
- Coarse sea salt to taste
- Freshly ground black pepper
- 2 cloves garlic
- Extra-virgin olive oil
- 2 sprigs rosemary
- 1 cup (250 milliliters) dry white wine
- 1 (12-ounce / 350-gram) ball Mixed Grain Pizza Dough (page 62)
- 2 red bell peppers, cored, seeded, and diced
- 4 green tomatoes, cut into ¼-inch (5-millimeter) slices
- 4 apricots, pitted and cut into small dice

Preheat the oven to 350°F (180°C).

To prepare the roast pork, rub the meat with salt, pepper, 1 clove garlic, and a small amount of oil. Mince the leaves of 1 of the sprigs of rosemary and massage them into the meat.

In an ovenproof pan over high heat brown the pork on all sides. Add the white wine and transfer the pan to the oven. Cook until the pork is cooked through, at least 45 minutes. To test for doneness, insert a metal skewer into the center of the roast. If the skewer is not very moist and is clean when you pull it out, the meat is cooked. Remove the pork from the oven and set aside to rest for 10 minutes.

Raise the oven temperature to 450°F to 475°F (220°C to 250°C). Stretch out the dough and place it in a well-oiled pan. Bake the pizza until golden brown and well risen, about 25 minutes.

While the pizza is baking, in a sauté pan over medium heat, sauté the bell peppers in a small amount of oil with the remaining garlic clove until softened. Grill or broil the green tomato slices until softened and slightly charred. Thinly slice the pork.

Remove the pizza from the oven and arrange the grilled tomatoes on the dough, topped by the sliced pork. Sprinkle the peppers and apricots over the top. Drizzle with a little oil. Strip the leaves from the remaining rosemary sprig and sprinkle them over the pizza. Serve hot.

Eggplant and Shrimp Pizza

- 1 (12-ounce / 350-gram) ball Mixed Grain Pizza Dough (page 62)
- Extra-virgin olive oil to taste
- 1½ pounds (700 grams) long narrow eggplant
- 2 cloves unpeeled garlic
- 1 chile
- Leaves of 1 bunch flat-leaf parsley, minced
- Fine sea salt to taste
- 2 pounds (1 kilogram) large shrimp in the shells
- ½ cup (125 milliliters) dry white wine
- Freshly ground black pepper to taste
- 10 ounces (300 grams) sun-dried tomatoes packed in oil, drained

Preheat the oven to 450°F to 475°F (220°C to 250°C).

Stretch out the dough and place it in a well-oiled pan. Thinly slice 2 of the eggplants into rounds and cover the entire surface of the dough with eggplant slices.

Bake the pizza until deep golden brown and well-risen, about 30 minutes.

While the pizza is baking, julienne the remaining eggplants. Place a small amount of oil, 1 garlic clove, and the chile in a sauté pan and cook over medium heat until the eggplant is soft. Discard the garlic and chile. Season with the parsley and salt.

Clean the shrimp (do not peel them) and cook them in a sauté pan with a small amount of oil and the remaining garlic clove. The shrimp will give off a little water, which will evaporate. As soon as it does, add the wine and a sprinkling of pepper and cook for 5 minutes more. Remove the shrimp from the pan. Peel half of the shrimp and leave the others in their shells.

Remove the pizza from the oven and arrange the cooked julienne eggplant on top of the eggplant slices. Top with the peeled shrimp, then the sun-dried tomatoes. Garnish with the unpeeled shrimp.

Pizza with Peppers and Ragusano Cheese

- 1 (12-ounce / 350-gram) ball White Pizza Dough (page 60)
- Extra-virgin olive oil to taste
- 1 pound (500 grams) red and yellow bell peppers, cored and seeded
- 12 ounces (350 grams) mozzarella
- 10 ounces (300 grams) Ragusano cheese (see Note), thinly sliced
- Oregano, preferably Sicilian oregano, to taste
- Fine sea salt to taste

Preheat the oven to 450°F to 475°F (220°C to 250°C).

Stretch out the dough and place it in a well-oiled pan. Cut the peppers into strips. Shred the mozzarella cheese by hand over the dough and scatter on the pepper strips. Drizzle with a little oil.

Bake the pizza until golden brown and well-risen, about 25 minutes, distributing the Ragusano cheese over the surface of the pizza about halfway through the cooking time.

Remove the pizza from the oven and sprinkle with the oregano. Season with salt and serve hot.

NOTE: *Ragusano is a seasoned pulled-curd cheese. It has an intense flavor and gives this pizza its particular character.*

Pizza with Three Tomatoes

- 1 pint (300 grams) grape tomatoes
- Extra-virgin olive oil to taste
- Fine sea salt to taste
- 10 ounces (300 grams) Casalino or other heirloom tomatoes
- Oregano to taste
- 1 clove unpeeled garlic
- 1 (12-ounce / 350-gram) ball Mixed Grain Pizza Dough (page 62)
- 1¼ cups (300 grams) canned peeled San Marzano tomatoes

Preheat the oven to 250°F (120°C).

Seed and chop the grape tomatoes. Season with oil and salt. Set aside.

Lightly oil a baking pan. Roughly chop the Casalino tomatoes and place them on the prepared pan. Season lightly with salt and oregano and add the garlic. Roast until extremely soft and concentrated, at least 3 hours. (If you prefer, you can preheat the oven to a higher temperature, then place the tomatoes in the oven, turn it off, and leave the tomatoes in the hot oven overnight.) Discard the garlic and puree the roasted tomatoes in a blender to create a smooth paste.

Raise the oven temperature to 450°F to 475°F (220°C to 250°C).

Stretch out the dough and place it in a well-oiled pan. Crush the canned tomatoes by hand into a small bowl. Toss with a little salt and oil, and spread over the dough.

Bake the pizza until golden brown and well-risen, about 25 minutes.

Remove the pizza from the oven and scatter the grape tomatoes and Casalino tomato puree over the top. Serve immediately.

Pizza with Squash Blossoms, Ricotta, and Black Olives

- 10 ounces (300 grams) fresh sheep's-milk ricotta
- 7 ounces (200 grams) black taggiasca olives (see Note), pitted and crushed
- 1 (12-ounce / 350-gram) ball White Pizza Dough (page 60)
- Extra-virgin olive oil to taste
- 9 ounces (250 grams) mozzarella
- 15 squash blossoms
- Fine sea salt to taste
- Freshly ground black pepper to taste

Preheat the oven to 450°F to 475°F (220°C to 250°C).

Mix the ricotta cheese and olives together to combine. Stretch out the dough and place it in a well-oiled pan. Tear the mozzarella cheese into pieces and scatter about half of it over the dough. Dot the dough with the ricotta and olive mixture. Place the whole squash blossoms on top. Scatter the remaining mozzarella cheese on top of the blossoms.

Bake the pizza until golden brown and well-risen, about 25 minutes.

Remove the pizza from the oven, season with salt and pepper, and drizzle with a little oil.

NOTE: *I prefer taggiasca olives for this pizza because these small olives from Liguria are sweet and delicate. A more bitter and intense variety, such as Gaeta olives, will overpower the taste of the squash blossoms. Taggiasca olives can be a little hard to track down in North America, but they're worth it.*

Pizza with Potatoes, Boiled Beef, and Mint

- 1 white onion
- 2 carrots
- 1 rib celery
- 2 whole cloves
- 4 bay leaves
- 1 bunch sage
- Coarse sea salt to taste
- 1 1-pound (500-gram) piece of beef
- Black peppercorns to taste
- 1 clove garlic
- 2 lemons
- 3½ ounces (100 grams) pine nuts
- Leaves of 1 bunch fresh mint
- 1 (12-ounce / 350-gram) ball White Pizza Dough (page 60)
- Extra-virgin olive oil to taste
- 1¾ pounds (800 grams) yellow potatoes, such as Yukon golds, boiled and peeled
- Freshly ground black pepper

Place the onion, carrots, celery, cloves, bay leaves, sage, and a handful of salt in a stockpot. Add cold water to cover. Bring to a boil, and when it's boiling add the meat. Reduce the heat and simmer for 1½ hours, until the meat is fork-tender.

Preheat the oven to 450°F to 475°F (220°C to 250°C).

With a mortar and pestle, grind together the peppercorns, garlic, the zest of ½ lemon (reserve the remaining lemon to zest on the completed pizza), the juice of the 2 lemons, the pine nuts, and the mint leaves (set aside a few of the prettiest leaves for garnish). Puree until the mixture forms a paste and set aside.

Stretch out the dough and place it in a well-oiled pan. With your hands, crush the boiled potatoes over the dough.

Bake the pizza until golden brown and well-risen, about 25 minutes.

Meanwhile, remove the boiled beef from the liquid. Slice the beef thinly and drizzle with a little oil.

Remove the pizza from the oven and arrange the beef on it in a single layer. Spread the pine nut mixture over the beef. Grate the zest of 1 lemon over the mixture. Season with pepper and garnish with the reserved mint leaves. Serve hot.

Anchovy Crostino with Zucchini and Peppers

- ½ cup (125 milliliters) white wine vinegar
- 10 salted anchovies
- Extra-virgin olive oil to taste
- 1 (12-ounce / 350-gram) ball White Pizza Dough (page 60)
- 9 ounces (250 grams) mozzarella
- 4 small zucchini
- 2 yellow peppers
- Leaves from 1 bunch oregano

Preheat the oven to 450°F to 475°F (220°C to 250°C).

Dilute the vinegar with ½ cup water. Scrape the salt off of the anchovies, bone them, and rinse them in the vinegar mixture. Pat them dry and drizzle them with a little oil.

Stretch out the dough and place it in a well-oiled pan. Arrange the anchovies on the dough in a single layer. Shred the cheese by hand on top of the anchovies. Thinly slice the zucchini and arrange the slices on top of the cheese. Seed and dice the peppers and scatter them on top.

Drizzle with a little oil and bake the pizza until golden brown and well-risen, about 25 minutes.

Remove the pizza from the oven, sprinkle with the oregano leaves, and serve warm or at room temperature.

Pizza with Tomato Sauce and Anchovies

- 1¾ pounds (800 grams) fresh anchovies
- 2 lemons
- Extra-virgin olive oil to taste
- 2 cups (500 milliliters) white wine vinegar
- 1 (12-ounce / 350-gram) ball White Pizza Dough (page 60)
- 2 cups (500 grams) canned peeled tomatoes
- Fine sea salt to taste
- 1 head garlic
- Freshly ground black pepper to taste
- ¼ cup loosely packed flat-leaf parsley leaves, minced

Preheat the oven to 450°F to 475°F (220°C to 250°C).

Clean, butterfly, and bone the anchovies. Arrange them in a nonreactive pan in a single layer. Zest ½ lemon and set aside for finishing the pizza. Juice both lemons, whisk the juice with a generous amount of oil and the vinegar, and pour the liquid over the fish. Cover and marinate until the flesh of the anchovies has turned white, about 20 minutes.

Stretch out the dough and place it in a well-oiled pan. In a small bowl, combine the tomatoes with some oil and salt. Spread the tomato mixture over the dough by hand, crushing the tomatoes between your fingers as you drop them onto the dough. Break up the garlic and scatter the unpeeled cloves over the tomato sauce.

Bake the pizza until golden brown and well-risen, about 25 minutes.

Remove the pizza from the oven and arrange the anchovies on top. Season with pepper, the reserved lemon zest, a drizzle of oil, and the parsley. Serve hot.

Pizza with Grouper and Scapece Zucchini

- 14 ounces (400 grams) grouper fillets, skinned
- Extra-virgin olive oil to taste
- 1 (12-ounce / 350-gram) ball White Pizza Dough (page 60)
- 14 ounces (400 grams) zucchini
- 2 cloves garlic, thinly sliced
- Leaves of 1 bunch wild mint
- 1 tablespoon white wine vinegar
- Fine sea salt to taste
- ¼ cup minced flat-leaf parsley

What is scapece*? In Rome, I always heard that the word scapece is derived from the Latin expression esca Apicii, or "dish of Apicio." Apicio or Apicius was the author of* De re Coquinaria (On the Subject of Cooking), *a collection of Roman recipes from the fourth or fifth century A.D. The story goes that the author was tired of* garum, *a kind of fermented anchovy condiment that was used liberally by Romans, so he invented a new vinegar-based sauce. In Liguria and Piedmont, they call this* scabeccio.

Preheat the oven to 450°F to 475°F (220°C to 250°C).

Cut the fish fillets into ½-inch (1½-centimeter) pieces. Toss the pieces with about 1 tablespoon oil.

Stretch out the dough and place it in a well-oiled pan. Scatter the fish pieces over the dough. Bake the pizza until the crust is golden brown and well-risen, about 25 minutes.

While the pizza is baking, cut the zucchini into thin slices (not paper-thin). Dry the slices thoroughly and fry them in a generous amount of oil in a skillet over medium heat until they are lightly browned on the edges. Remove the fried zucchini slices from the oil and spread them on paper towels to drain. Place the fried zucchini slices in a bowl, scatter on the garlic and mint, then drizzle with the vinegar. Season with oil and salt and toss to combine.

Remove the pizza from the oven, distribute the zucchini slices evenly over the surface, and sprinkle with the minced parsley.

Pizza with Green Tomatoes, Mango, Baccalà, and Bitter Greens

- 1 (12-ounce / 350-gram) ball White Pizza Dough (page 60)
- Extra-virgin olive oil to taste
- 10 ounces (300 grams) green tomatoes
- Fine sea salt to taste
- Freshly ground black pepper to taste
- 10 ounces (300 grams) baccalà, soaked in water to cover in the refrigerator for 1 to 3 days, with the water changed 3 times a day, then rinsed thoroughly
- 1 ripe mango
- Juice of 1 lemon
- 1 bunch arugula
- 1 bunch dandelion greens
- 1 bunch chicory greens

Preheat the oven to 450°F to 475°F (220°C to 250°C).

Stretch out the dough and place it in a well-oiled pan. Slice the green tomatoes using a mandoline and distribute the slices in a single layer over the dough to cover it completely. Season with salt and pepper.

Bake the pizza on the bottom shelf of the oven until golden brown and well-risen, about 25 minutes.

Remove the pizza from the oven and set aside to cool slightly.

Meanwhile, cut the baccalà very thinly diagonal to the grain. Peel the mango, dice it, and toss it with the lemon juice and about 1 tablespoon oil. Tear the greens into small pieces if they are large.

Distribute the sliced baccalà over the green tomatoes. Scatter on the diced mango and greens. Serve warm.

Pizza with Prosciutto Cotto and Bell Pepper Puree

- 2 pounds (1 kilogram) red and yellow bell peppers
- 1 cup (250 milliliters) extra-virgin olive oil, plus more to taste
- 1 tablespoon apple cider vinegar
- 1 (12-ounce / 350-gram) ball White Pizza Dough (page 60)
- 9 ounces (250 grams) thinly sliced prosciutto cotto

Leave the peppers whole and broil them, turning occasionally, until charred on all sides. Transfer the peppers to a clean plastic bag and seal the bag. Let the peppers cool. When they are cool enough to handle, peel them, seed them, and cut them into strips. Place the pepper strips in a bowl with the 1 cup (250 milliliters) oil and puree using an immersion blender (or a stand blender). Add the vinegar and puree until perfectly smooth.

Preheat the oven to 450°F to 475°F (220°C to 250°C).

Stretch out the dough and place it in a well-oiled pan.

Bake the pizza until golden brown and well-risen, about 25 minutes.

Remove the pizza from the oven, distribute the prosciutto cotto slices on top of the dough, and top with the pepper puree just before serving.

Uncle Pietro Uncle's Pizza

- 1 (12-ounce / 350-gram) ball White Pizza Dough (page 60)
- Extra-virgin olive oil to taste
- 1 pound (500 grams) zucchini (see Note)
- 10 ounces (300 grams) sheep's-milk ricotta
- Fine sea salt to taste
- Freshly ground black pepper to taste
- Grated nutmeg to taste

I have an uncle I adore who has a habit of repeating words at the start and end of every sentence. He did it once when ordering a pizza that I make with both raw and cooked zucchini, so I named the recipe for him.

Preheat the oven to 450°F to 475°F (220°C to 250°C).

Stretch out the dough and place it in a well-oiled pan. Slice the zucchini very thinly (a mandoline works well) and arrange about two-thirds of the zucchini slices in a single layer on the dough, reserving the rest.

Bake the pizza until golden brown and well-risen, about 25 minutes.

Remove the pizza from the oven and let it cool for at least 5 minutes. Distribute the ricotta on top of the cooked zucchini, then place the raw zucchini slices on top of the cheese. Season with salt, pepper, and nutmeg.

NOTE: *For this recipe, I use a special Roman variety of zucchini with a ridged exterior. If you cannot find this variety, then seek out small zucchini that look very fresh.*

Pizza with Grilled Peaches and Curly Endive

- 1 (12-ounce / 350-gram) ball White Pizza Dough (page 60)
- Extra-virgin olive oil to taste
- 7 ounces (200 grams) yellow potatoes, such as Yukon golds, boiled and peeled
- Fine sea salt to taste
- 1¾ pounds (800 grams) curly endive
- 1 unpeeled clove garlic
- 1 fresh chile, halved
- 3 yellow peaches

Preheat the oven to 450°F to 475°F (220°C to 250°C).

Stretch out the dough and place it in a well-oiled pan. Crush the potatoes between your fingers and let them fall onto the pizza dough.

Bake the pizza until deep golden brown and well-risen, about 30 minutes.

While the pizza is baking, blanch the greens in a saucepan of boiling salted water. Drain, squeeze out as much water as possible, chop coarsely, and sauté over medium heat in a sauté pan in a small amount of oil with the garlic and chile, just until heated through. Remove and discard the whole garlic clove and chile.

Heat a grill or grill pan or broiler. Pit and peel the peaches and cut them into ¼-inch (½-centimeter) slices. Grill them until they have charred grill marks.

Remove the pizza from the oven. Distribute the grilled peaches on top of the potatoes and top with the sautéed greens.

Spicy Pizza with Eggplant and Burrata

- 1 (12-ounce / 350-gram) ball White Pizza Dough (page 60)
- Extra-virgin olive oil to taste
- 1 pound (500 grams) eggplant
- Fine sea salt to taste
- 10 ounces (300 grams) burrata (see Note), chopped
- Red chile flakes to taste

Preheat the oven to 450°F to 475°F (220°C to 250°C).

Stretch out the dough and place it in a well-oiled pan. Thinly slice the eggplant into rounds and toss them with a small amount of oil and salt. Arrange the eggplant rounds on top of the dough.

Bake the pizza until golden brown and well-risen, about 25 minutes.

Remove the pizza from the oven and arrange the cheese on top. Sprinkle with chile flakes.

NOTE: *Burrata is an even creamier version of mozzarella from Puglia. It should be utterly fresh. If you have more burrata than you need for this recipe, use the creamy center rather than the stiffer outer shell.*

Pizza with Potatoes, Green Beans, and Sautéed Cuttlefish

- 1 (12-ounce / 350-gram) ball White Pizza Dough (page 60)
- Extra-virgin olive oil to taste
- 14 ounces (400 grams) yellow potatoes, such as Yukon golds, boiled and peeled
- 1 pound (500 grams) green beans, trimmed
- Fine sea salt to taste
- 1 pound (500 grams) medium cuttlefish, cleaned
- 1 unpeeled clove garlic
- ½ cup (125 milliliters) dry white wine
- Freshly ground black pepper
- Grated zest of 1 lemon

Preheat the oven to 450°F to 475°F (220°C to 250°C).

Stretch out the dough and place it in a well-oiled pan. Crush the potatoes between your fingers and let them fall onto the pizza dough.

Bake the pizza until golden brown and well-risen, about 25 minutes.

While the pizza is baking, blanch the green beans in a saucepan of boiling salted water. Cut the cuttlefish into strips. Heat a tablespoon or two of oil in a sauté pan over high heat, add the garlic, and sauté until softened. Add the cuttlefish and cook for 3 minutes. Add the white wine and a pinch of salt. Remove and discard the garlic.

Remove the pizza from the oven and scatter the green beans and cuttlefish on top. Season with pepper and scatter on the lemon zest.

Shrimp Cocktail Pizza

- 1 yellow onion, minced
- ¾ cup (200 milliliters) extra-virgin olive oil, plus more to taste
- 1 apple, peeled, cored, and minced
- 2 cups (500 grams) tomato puree
- 1 red bell pepper, cored, seeded, and chopped
- 2 tablespoons granulated sugar
- 1 cup (250 milliliters) apple cider vinegar
- 2 whole cloves
- 2 large eggs, at room temperature
- 1 (12-ounce / 350-gram) ball Mixed Grain Pizza Dough (page 62)
- 2 cups (500 grams) canned peeled tomatoes
- 10 large shrimp
- 1 head frisée

MAKE THE KETCHUP: In a medium saucepan, sauté the onion in a small amount of oil over medium heat until softened. Add the apple, tomato puree, bell pepper, sugar, vinegar, and cloves. Bring to a simmer and simmer until thickened, about 1 hour. Remove and discard the cloves, then puree the entire mixture in a blender and set aside to cool. (This is more ketchup than you will need for this recipe, but if you place the remaining ketchup in a clean jar and refrigerate it, it will last for up to 1 week.)

MAKE THE MAYONNAISE: Emulsify the eggs with the ¾ cup (200 milliliters) oil. An immersion blender is the best tool for the job.

MAKE THE COCKTAIL SAUCE: Combine about 1½ cups (300 grams) of the mayonnaise with 3 tablespoons of the ketchup.

When you are ready to bake the pizza, preheat the oven to 450°F to 475°F (220°C to 250°C).

Stretch out the dough and place it in a well-oiled pan. Crush the canned peeled tomatoes and scatter them onto the dough.

Bake the pizza until golden brown and well-risen, about 25 minutes.

While the pizza is baking, in a sauté pan over medium heat, cook the shrimp in a small amount of oil until just pink, about 5 minutes. Shell and devein the cooked shrimp, but leave them whole.

Remove the pizza from the oven and tear the frisée leaves over it, letting them fall on top of the tomatoes. Top with the cocktail sauce and the warm shrimp.

AUTUMN PIZZAS

Pizza with Tomatoes and Baccalà

- 1 (12-ounce / 350-gram) ball White Pizza Dough (page 60)
- Extra-virgin olive oil to taste
- 1¼ cups (300 grams) canned peeled tomatoes
- Fine sea salt to taste
- 1 pound (500 grams) baccalà, soaked in water to cover in the refrigerator for 1 to 3 days, with the water changed 3 times a day, then rinsed thoroughly
- 7 ounces (200 grams) sun-dried tomatoes
- Leaves of 1 bunch basil
- 1⅛ cups (200 grams) blanched almonds

Preheat the oven to 450°F to 475°F (220°C to 250°C).

Stretch out the dough and place it in a well-oiled pan. In a bowl, toss the peeled tomatoes with some oil and salt, then crush them through your fingers onto the surface of the dough. Rub them all over the dough.

Bake the pizza for 20 minutes until golden brown.

While the pizza is baking, remove any bones from the baccalà and thinly slice it (like for carpaccio). When the pizza has baked for 20 minutes, distribute the raw baccalà on top of the dough and drizzle with some oil. Return to the oven and bake for an additional 10 minutes.

In a mortar and pestle or blender, grind the sun-dried tomatoes, basil leaves, and almonds to a paste.

Remove the pizza from the oven. Spread the paste on top of the pizza, and serve immediately.

Pizza with Mushrooms

- 10 ounces (300 grams) porcini mushrooms
- 10 ounces (300 grams) white button mushrooms
- 10 ounces (300 grams) chanterelle mushrooms
- 10 ounces (300 grams) black poplar mushrooms
- Extra-virgin olive oil to taste
- 3 cloves garlic
- Fine sea salt to taste
- Freshly ground black pepper to taste
- 1 (12-ounce / 350-gram) ball White Pizza Dough (page 60)
- 1¼ cups (300 grams) canned peeled tomatoes
- Mint leaves (optional)

Preheat the oven to 450°F to 475°F (220°C to 250°C).

Clean all the mushrooms with a damp cloth or a small soft brush to remove any soil clinging to them. Take care not to damage them.

Thinly slice the porcini and button mushrooms. Halve the chanterelles and black poplar mushrooms. Heat a little oil in a sauté pan. Peel the garlic and add it to the pan. When the oil is hot, add all of the mushrooms to the pan. Season with salt and pepper and sauté for just 3 minutes. The mushrooms should remain firm.

Stretch out the dough and place it in a well-oiled pan. In a bowl, toss the tomatoes with some oil and salt, then crush them through your fingers onto the surface of the dough.

Bake the pizza until golden brown and well-risen, about 25 minutes.

Remove the pizza from the oven and distribute the mushrooms on top. Garnish with mint leaves, if using, and serve.

Pizza Stuffed with Broccolini and Mortadella

- 2 (12-ounce / 350-gram) balls White Pizza Dough (page 60)
- Extra-virgin olive oil to taste
- 14 ounces (400 grams) broccolini
- Fine sea salt to taste
- 10 ounces (300 grams) thinly sliced mortadella
- Lemon juice (optional)

Preheat the oven to 450°F to 475°F (220°C to 250°C).

MAKE A "DOUBLE" PIZZA: Stretch out 1 ball of dough and place it in a well-oiled pan. Brush the top of the dough with additional oil.

Chop the broccolini, toss it with oil and salt, and scatter it over the dough in the pan. On a lightly floured surface, stretch out the second ball of dough and place it gently on top of the broccolini.

Bake the pizza for 30 minutes, until golden brown and well-risen. At this point, the broccolini should be cooked inside the pizza.

Remove the pizza from the oven and gently stuff the mortadella between the 2 layers. If you like, drizzle on some lemon juice; it adds an interesting dimension.

Pizza with Ricotta, Persimmons, and 'Nduja

- 1 (12-ounce / 350-gram) ball White Pizza Dough (page 60)
- Extra-virgin olive oil to taste
- 1 pound (500 grams) sheep's-milk ricotta
- 1 pound (500 grams) 'Nduja sausage (see Note)
- 4 very ripe persimmons
- Fine sea salt to taste
- 1 cup (150 grams) Alba or other hazelnuts, toasted and chopped

Preheat the oven to 450°F to 475°F (220°C to 250°C).

Stretch out the dough and place it in a well-oiled pan.

Bake until golden brown and well-risen, about 25 minutes.

Remove the pizza from the oven and drop the ricotta on top with a spoon (do not press). Cut the 'Nduja into large pieces (about the size of a walnut) and intersperse them among the pieces of ricotta. Slice the persimmons and distribute them on top of the ricotta in between the pieces of 'Nduja. Season with salt and sprinkle with the hazelnuts.

NOTE: *'Nduja is a very soft, spreadable cured meat from the Spilinga area of Calabria made using pork trimmings and spicy chiles. There is no real substitute for it, but unfortunately it is not currently available in the United States. You can replace it with spicy sausage, or try making your own if you're ambitious.*

Pizza with Gruyère and Chicory

- 1 pound (500 grams) chicory
- Fine sea salt to taste
- Extra-virgin olive oil to taste
- 1 clove garlic
- Red chile flakes
- 1 (12-ounce / 350-gram) ball White Pizza Dough (page 60)
- 10 ounces (300 grams) Gruyère, thinly sliced

Preheat the oven to 450°F to 475°F (220°C to 250°C).

Blanch the chicory in a saucepan of boiling salted water. Drain, squeeze dry, chop, and sauté over medium heat in a small amount of oil with the garlic clove and a pinch of chile flakes, just until heated through.

Stretch out the dough and place it in a well-oiled pan.

Bake until golden brown and well-risen, about 25 minutes.

Remove the pizza from the oven, scatter the cheese on top, and add the cooked greens. Serve hot.

Smoked Pizza

- 1 (12-ounce / 350-gram) ball White Pizza Dough (page 60)
- Extra-virgin olive oil to taste
- 1 pound (500 grams) yellow potatoes, such as Yukon golds, boiled and peeled
- 1 pound (500 grams) smoked buffalo mozzarella or other smoked mozzarella, sliced
- 7 ounces (200 grams) sliced speck (see Note)
- Leaves of 1 bunch thyme

Preheat the oven to 450°F to 475°F (220°C to 250°C).

Stretch out the dough and place it in a well-oiled pan. Crush the potatoes between your fingers and let them fall onto the dough. Drizzle with a little more oil.

Bake the pizza until golden brown and well-risen, about 25 minutes.

Remove the pizza from the oven and distribute the cheese over the surface of the dough, topped by the speck and then the thyme leaves. Drizzle with a little oil and serve warm.

NOTE: *Speck is a smoked pork shoulder that is cured using juniper berries and other spices. For this recipe, opt for a high-quality speck without too much salt and with a light touch when it comes to smoking.*

Pizza with Shrimp and Porcini Mushrooms

- 1 (12-ounce / 350-gram) ball White Pizza Dough (page 60)
- Extra-virgin olive oil to taste
- 1 pound (500 grams) porcini mushrooms
- 1 unpeeled clove garlic
- Fine sea salt to taste
- Freshly ground black pepper to taste
- 10 large shrimp, 1½ to 1¾ pounds (700 to 800 grams) total
- 1 chile
- ½ cup (125 milliliters) dry white wine
- Minced mint leaves to taste

Preheat the oven to 450°F to 475°F (220°C to 250°C).

Stretch out the dough and place it in a well-oiled pan.

Bake the pizza until golden brown and well-risen, about 25 minutes.

While the pizza is baking, clean the mushrooms with a damp cloth or a soft brush, but do not soak. Thinly slice the caps and mince the stems. In a sauté pan, cook the mushrooms in 1 tablespoon oil with the garlic over high heat until cooked through but still firm, 4 to 5 minutes. Remove and discard the garlic. Season the mushrooms with salt and pepper. Remove from the pan with a slotted spoon and set aside.

In the same pan, cook the shrimp with the chile. As soon as the shrimp begin to turn pink, add the wine and cook for 8 to 10 minutes. Remove the cooked shrimp from the pan, peel them, and return them very briefly to the pan to moisten. Remove and discard the chile.

Remove the pizza from the oven and distribute the mushrooms over the top. (Reserve a few slices of the caps for garnish if you like.) Scatter on the mint. Top with the hot shrimp and serve immediately.

Focaccia with Grapes

- 1⅓ pounds (600 grams) small green grapes
- 1 (12-ounce / 350-gram) ball Mixed Grain Pizza Dough (page 62)
- Extra-virgin olive oil to taste

Preheat the oven to 450°F to 475°F (220°C to 250°C).

Wash the grapes thoroughly and remove them from the stems. Cut each grape in half and remove the seeds.

Stretch out the dough and place it in a well-oiled pan. Scatter the grapes over the dough.

Bake the pizza until deep golden brown and well-risen, about 30 minutes.

Remove the pizza from the oven and serve hot.

NOTE: *This type of focaccia is perfect for serving with both fresh and aged cheeses.*

Look for Pizzutella grapes, cylindrical green table grapes that remain firm and flavorful even after baking.

Pizza with Mashed Potatoes and Cotechino Sausage

- 2 pounds (1 kilogram) yellow potatoes, such as Yukon golds
- 7 tablespoons (100 grams) unsalted butter
- Fine sea salt to taste
- 1 (12-ounce / 350-gram) ball White Pizza Dough (page 60)
- Extra-virgin olive oil to taste
- 1 14-ounce (400-gram) cotechino sausage (see Note)

Preheat the oven to 450°F to 475°F (220°C to 250°C).

Boil the potatoes, and while they are still warm, peel them and place them in a bowl with the butter; mash the potatoes with a fork until smooth. Season lightly with salt.

Stretch out the dough and place it in a well-oiled pan. Spread the mashed potatoes on it in an even layer and bake the pizza for 25 minutes.

While the pizza is baking, cook the cotechino in a saucepan of boiling water to cover until it is firm (but do not puncture it with a fork). Drain the sausage and let it cool. Cut it into ½-inch-thick (1-centimeter) slices.

Remove the pizza from the oven and let it cool until it is still warm but no longer piping hot. Arrange the cotechino slices on the pizza and serve.

NOTE: *Cotechino is a type of fresh pork sausage that is a specialty of the Emilia-Romagna region. It has a soft texture and usually contains pork rind.*

Pizza with Chicory, Rabbit, and Grapes

- Extra-virgin olive oil to taste
- 2 unpeeled cloves garlic
- 1 salted anchovy, rinsed, boned, and minced
- 1 (2-pound / 1-kilogram) rabbit, boned and chopped
- Leaves of 1 sprig rosemary, minced
- Leaves of 1 bunch thyme, minced
- Leaves of 1 bunch sage, minced
- Fine sea salt to taste
- Freshly ground black pepper to taste
- 1 cup (250 milliliters) dry white wine
- 1½ pounds (600 grams) green grapes
- 1 (12-ounce / 350-gram) ball Mixed Grain Pizza Dough (page 62)
- 1 pound (500 grams) chicory

Preheat the oven to 450°F to 475°F (220°C to 250°C).

In a pot, preferably a terra-cotta pot, heat a tablespoon or so of oil over high heat and add 1 clove garlic and the anchovy. Add the rabbit and brown it on all sides. Add the herbs to the rabbit, season with salt and pepper, and add the wine. Turn the heat down and simmer for 35 minutes. Remove and discard the garlic.

Meanwhile, remove the grapes from their stems, slice each grape in half, and remove the seeds.

Stretch out the dough and place it in a well-oiled pan. Scatter the grapes on the surface of the dough.

Bake the pizza until deep golden brown and well-risen, about 30 minutes.

While the pizza is baking, blanch the chicory in a saucepan of boiling salted water. Chop the greens and sauté in 1 tablespoon of oil with the remaining 1 clove garlic for a couple minutes. Remove and discard the garlic.

Remove the pizza from the oven and distribute the chicory on the surface. Top the greens with the pieces of rabbit and serve immediately.

Focaccia with Chestnut, Porcini, Squab, and Radish

- 1 squab, cleaned and gutted
- Extra-virgin olive oil to taste
- 4 cloves garlic, peeled
- 2 bay leaves
- 1 sprig rosemary
- 30 chestnuts
- 1 (12-ounce / 350-gram) ball Mixed Grain Pizza Dough (page 62)
- 5 porcini mushrooms, thinly sliced
- Leaves of 1 bunch thyme
- 10 ounces (300 grams) radishes, minced
- Fine sea salt to taste

Preheat the oven to 450°F to 475°F (220°C to 250°C).

In a saucepan, cook the squab in 1 tablespoon oil with 3 cloves of the garlic, 1 bay leaf, and the rosemary over high heat until nicely browned on all sides. Reduce the heat to low and cook until cooked through, about 30 minutes. Remove from the heat and let rest for at least 15 minutes, then carefully cut the 2 breast halves and 2 thighs from the squab. Bone the breast and thighs and slice them. Discard the garlic, bay leaves, and rosemary.

Cook the chestnuts in a saucepan of boiling water with the remaining bay leaf for at least 15 minutes, until cooked through but still firm. Don't overcook. Remove them with a slotted spoon (reserve the cooking water), peel them, and remove their skins. Pass the cooked chestnuts through a ricer or food mill and then a sieve, add ¼ cup to ½ cup of the cooking water and a few drops of oil. Whisk until smooth.

Stretch out the dough and place it in a well-oiled pan. Bake the pizza until golden brown and well-risen, about 25 minutes.

While the pizza is baking, cook the mushrooms over medium heat with the remaining clove of garlic and the thyme leaves in a small skillet in a small amount of oil, until the mushrooms are softened.

Remove the pizza from the oven and spread the chestnut puree on top. Alternate slices of the squab and the mushrooms over the puree. Scatter on the minced radishes. Season with oil, salt, and pepper and serve hot.

Pizza with Squash, Grana, and Amaretto Cookies

- 1 pound (500 grams) Mantovana squash or another squash with very dry flesh
- Extra-virgin olive oil to taste
- Fine sea salt to taste
- Grated nutmeg to taste
- 1 (12-ounce / 350-gram) ball White Pizza Dough (page 60)
- 7 ounces (200 grams) grana cheese
- 7 ounces (200 grams) amaretti cookies (see Note), crushed
- Freshly ground black pepper to taste

Preheat the oven to 350°F (180°C).

Seed the squash and cut it onto thick slices. Line a baking sheet with parchment and arrange the squash slices on it in a single layer. Bake until soft, about 30 minutes. Scoop out the cooked squash flesh with a spoon. Puree the squash in a blender with a drizzle of oil, a pinch of salt, and a pinch of grated nutmeg.

Raise the oven temperature to 450°F to 475°F (220°C to 250°C).

Stretch out the dough and place it in a well-oiled pan.

Bake the pizza until golden brown and well-risen, about 25 minutes.

Spread the squash puree over the surface of the pizza. Shave the cheese over the pizza and sprinkle the crushed cookies on top. Season with salt and pepper and serve.

You can replace the more common almond amaretto cookies with hazelnut cookies, which are lighter and often more crumbly than the almond type. You can leave them whole if you like, because they're very small (as shown in the photo). Grana is a term for any hard, grainy cheese, such as Parmigiano-Reggiano.

Pizza with Tuna-style Tongue and Pickled Vegetables

- 1½ quarts (1½ liters) white wine vinegar
- 2 bay leaves
- Coarse sea salt to taste
- 2 pounds (1 kilogram) beef tongue
- Extra-virgin olive oil to taste
- Black peppercorns to taste
- 1 (12-ounce / 350-gram) ball Mixed Grain Pizza Dough (page 62)
- 3 carrots, cut into julienne
- 1 rib celery, cut into julienne
- 5 ounces (150 grams) pearl onions, peeled
- 7 ounces (200 grams) Romanesco broccoli, cut into florets
- 7 ounces (200 grams) cauliflower, cut into florets
- 7 ounces (200 grams) piquillo peppers (see Note, page 241)
- ¼ cup loosely packed flat-leaf parsley leaves, minced

Fill a large pot with 2 quarts (2 liters) of water, 3 cups (750 milliliters) of the white wine vinegar, 1 bay leaf, and a handful of coarse sea salt. Bring to a boil, add the tongue, and cook at a simmer for 1 hour. Turn off the heat and leave the tongue in the liquid until it has cooled to room temperature. Remove the tongue from the water and cool completely.

Remove the membrane from the tongue. Cut the meat into ¼-inch (5-millimeter) slices and place them in a jar. Add oil to cover the tongue along with a few black peppercorns and close the jar.

Preheat the oven to 450°F to 475°F (220°C to 250°C).

Stretch out the dough and place it in a well-oiled pan.

Bake the pizza until golden brown and well-risen, about 25 minutes.

Meanwhile, fill a clean pot with 2 quarts (2 liters) of water, the remaining 3 cups (750 milliliters) vinegar, the remaining bay leaf, and a handful of coarse sea salt. Bring to a boil, then add the carrots, celery, onions, broccoli, and cauliflower and blanch for 5 minutes. Drain.

Remove the pizza from the oven and let it cool until it is warm but no longer piping hot. Remove the tongue slices from the oil and drain them briefly, then arrange them on the pizza. Top with the pickled vegetables and the peppers. Drizzle with a little additional oil and sprinkle with the parsley.

Pizza with Piennolo Tomatoes, Romanesco Broccoli, and Caciocavallo Cheese

- 1 (12-ounce / 350-gram) ball White Pizza Dough (page 60)
- Extra-virgin olive oil to taste
- 1 pound (500 grams) Romanesco broccoli
- Fine sea salt to taste
- 1 fresh chile
- 1 unpeeled clove garlic
- 10 ounces (300 grams) Piennolo tomatoes (see Note)
- 7 ounces (200 grams) caciocavallo cheese, sliced
- Freshly ground black pepper to taste

Preheat the oven to 450°F to 475°F (220°C to 250°C).

Stretch out the dough and place it in a well-oiled pan.

Bake the pizza until golden brown and well-risen, about 25 minutes.

While the pizza is baking, blanch the broccoli in a saucepan of lightly salted boiling water; drain.

Crush the cooked broccoli into chunks and sauté quickly in a skillet with a little oil, the chile, and the garlic. Remove and discard chile and garlic.

Char the tomatoes on a griddle or in a very hot cast-iron pan.

Remove the pizza from the oven, spread the broccoli on top, then the cheese, and then the tomatoes. Drizzle on a little more oil and season with pepper. Serve warm.

Piennolo tomatoes are lovely flavorful tomatoes grown on Vesuvius. They are also known as spongilli or piennoli, which is dialect for pendoli, or hangers, because they sometimes hang from the walls and ceilings. You can use other small cherry or grape tomatoes in their place.

Pizza with Black Poplar Mushrooms, Grana, and Cured Beef

- ½ cup (175 grams) coarse sea salt
- ½ cup (125 grams) sugar
- 12 ounces (350 grams) beef filet
- 1 sprig rosemary
- 1 (12-ounce / 350-gram) ball White Pizza Dough (page 60)
- Extra-virgin olive oil to taste
- 1¼ cups (300 grams) canned peeled tomatoes
- Fine sea salt to taste
- 7 ounces (200 grams) black poplar mushrooms, sliced
- 1 unpeeled clove garlic
- 3½ ounces (100 grams) grana cheese

Use an immersion blender to combine 3 cups (750 milliliters) water, the coarse salt, and sugar. When the salt and sugar have dissolved, set the meat in this brine, add the rosemary, and marinate in the refrigerator, covered, for 24 hours. Remove the meat, pat it dry, and cut it into thin slices—using a meat slicer if possible.

Preheat the oven to 450°F to 475°F (220°C to 250°C).

Stretch out the dough and place it in a well-oiled pan. Crush the tomatoes by hand onto the dough and season with fine sea salt.

Bake the pizza until golden brown and well-risen, about 25 minutes.

While the pizza is baking, in a medium sauté pan, sauté the mushrooms with a small amount of oil and the garlic over medium heat for 5 minutes. Remove and discard the garlic.

Remove the pizza from the oven and arrange the slices of cured beef on top. Scatter the mushrooms on top, then shave the cheese over them. Serve very hot.

Pizza with Oranges, Spinach, and Coppa di Testa

- 4 oranges, preferably organic
- 1 (12-ounce / 350-gram) ball White Pizza Dough (page 60)
- Extra-virgin olive oil to taste
- 1 pound (500 grams) spinach
- 1 unpeeled clove garlic
- Fine sea salt to taste
- Freshly ground black pepper to taste
- 10 ounces (300 grams) thin slices coppa di testa (Italian pork head cheese)

Preheat the oven to 450°F to 475°F (220°C to 250°C).

Slice the unpeeled oranges very thinly, using a mandoline or meat slicer if possible.

Stretch out the dough and place it in a well-oiled pan. Distribute the orange slices on top of the dough.

Bake the pizza until golden brown and well-risen, about 25 minutes.

While the pizza is baking, in a large sauté pan, briefly sauté the spinach in a small amount of oil with the garlic clove over medium heat. Season with salt and pepper.

Remove the pizza from the oven and set aside to rest for at least 5 minutes.

Remove and discard the garlic from the spinach and arrange the spinach on top of the oranges. Top with the coppa.

Pizza with Turnips and Squid

- 4 white turnips with leaves attached
- 1 (12-ounce / 350-gram) ball Whole Grain Pizza Dough (page 64)
- Extra-virgin olive oil to taste
- 1 clove garlic
- 5 medium squid, cleaned
- 1 chile, seeded
- ½ cup (125 milliliters) dry white wine
- Fine sea salt to taste
- Zest of 1 lemon
- Freshly ground black pepper to taste

Preheat the oven to 450°F to 475°F (220°C to 250°C).

Cut off and reserve a few tender turnip leaves. Peel the turnips and cut them into very thin slices.

Stretch out the dough and place it in a well-oiled pan. Distribute the turnip slices on top of the dough and brush a generous amount of oil on the turnips and the dough.

Bake the pizza until deep golden brown and well-risen, about 30 minutes.

Place a small amount of oil in a sauté pan and sauté the squid with the chile over medium heat until the squid turn opaque, about 2 minutes. Add the wine to the pan, season with salt, and cook until the wine has evaporated, no longer than 10 minutes.

Remove the pizza from the oven. Cut the squid into medium pieces and distribute them on top of the pizza. Sprinkle the lemon zest over the squid and garnish with the reserved turnip leaves. Season with pepper and serve piping hot.

Pizza with Turnips, Veal, and Chestnuts

- 1 pound (500 grams) veal stew meat, such as neck and shoulder
- Fine sea salt to taste
- Freshly ground black pepper to taste
- Extra-virgin olive oil to taste
- 1 unpeeled clove garlic
- White wine as needed
- 1 bunch sage
- 1 bunch flat-leaf parsley
- 2 bay leaves
- 1 onion
- 1 carrot
- 1 rib celery
- 10 chestnuts
- 4 white turnips
- 1 (12-ounce / 350-gram) ball Whole Grain Pizza Dough (page 64)
- Lemon juice to taste

Season the meat with salt and pepper, then brown it in a saucepan in a small amount of oil with the garlic clove. Add wine to cover, along with the sage, parsley, bay leaves, onion, carrot, and celery. (Leave the vegetables whole, or chop the carrots and celery if they don't fit into your pot.) Bring to a boil, then reduce the heat and simmer until the meat is fork-tender, at least 2½ hours. If the liquid boils off too quickly and the pot looks dry, add wine, water, or stock as needed.

When you are ready to bake the pizza, preheat the oven to 450°F to 475°F (220°C to 250°C).

Place the chestnuts in a hot cast-iron pan without cutting the shells and toast for 5 minutes. Remove the chestnuts from the heat and let them cool, then peel them with a paring knife.

Cut off and reserve a few tender turnip leaves. Peel the turnips and cut them into very thin slices. Stretch out the dough and place it in a well-oiled pan. Distribute the turnip slices on top of the dough. Brush a generous amount of oil on the turnips and the dough. Bake the pizza until deep golden brown and well-risen, about 30 minutes.

Meanwhile, cut the stewed veal into slices. (It will probably shred into small pieces.) Chop the turnip leaves and toss them with a small amount of oil and some lemon juice. Thinly slice the chestnuts using a shaver.

Remove the pizza from the oven and immediately arrange the stewed meat on top of the turnips. Scatter on the turnip leaves and place the chestnut slices on top. Serve warm.

Pizza with Winter Squash, Pancetta, and Provolone

- 2 pounds (1 kilogram) Mantovana squash or another squash with very dry flesh
- Extra-virgin olive oil to taste
- Fine sea salt to taste
- 1 (12-ounce / 350-gram) ball Mixed Grain Pizza Dough (page 62)
- 10 ounces (300 grams) smoked provolone cheese, sliced ½ inch (1 centimeter) thick
- 10 ounces (300 grams) pancetta slices

Preheat the oven to 400°F (200°C).

Seed the squash and cut it into thick slices. Line a baking sheet with parchment and arrange the squash slices on it in a single layer. Bake until very soft, about 45 minutes. Scoop out the cooked squash flesh with a spoon. Puree the squash in a blender with a drizzle of oil, a pinch of salt, and ½ cup (125 milliliters) hot water.

Raise the oven temperature to 450°F to 475°F (220°C to 250°C).

Stretch out the dough and place it in a well-oiled pan. Spread the squash puree on the dough.

Bake the pizza until deep golden brown and well-risen, about 30 minutes.

Remove the pizza from the oven and immediately arrange the cheese slices on top in a single layer. Place the pancetta on top of the cheese and serve piping hot.

This pizza is dedicated to Angelo Iezzi, a Roman pizza maker and the winner of the World Pizza Championship. He has served as my role model and was a great help to me, especially at the beginning of my career in pizza.

WINTER PIZZAS

Pizza with Beans and Sausage

- 10 ounces (300 grams) dried cranberry beans
- Extra-virgin olive oil to taste
- 1 clove garlic
- 1 rib celery
- Fine sea salt to taste
- 1 (12-ounce / 350-gram) ball White Pizza Dough (page 60)
- 4 pork sausages with finely ground stuffing, roughly chopped
- ¼ cup loosely packed flat-leaf parsley leaves, minced
- 4 to 5 tender celery leaves, minced
- Freshly ground black pepper to taste

Soak the beans overnight in cold water to cover. The next day, drain the beans, place them in a pot with water to cover, the garlic, and the celery (roughly chopped if necessary for it to fit into the pan). Bring to a boil, reduce the heat, and simmer until soft enough that you can crush a bean between your tongue and your palate, about 45 minutes. (Test 4 or 5 beans—they can vary in doneness.) Drain the beans and puree them in a blender with a tablespoon or so of oil and some salt.

When you are ready to bake the pizza, preheat the oven to 450°F to 475°F (220°C to 250°C).

Stretch out the dough and place it in a well-oiled pan. Scatter the chopped sausage over the dough.

Bake the pizza until deep golden brown and well-risen, about 30 minutes.

Remove the pizza from the oven and spread the bean puree on top. Sprinkle with the parsley and celery leaves. Season with black pepper (and a little salt, if needed—this will depend on how salty the sausage is) and serve immediately.

Pizza with Chicory

- 2 (12-ounce / 350-gram) balls Mixed Grain Pizza Dough (page 62)
- Extra-virgin olive oil to taste
- 1⅓ pounds (600 grams) chicory or other bitter greens
- Fine sea salt to taste
- 1 clove garlic, minced
- 1 fresh chile, minced

Preheat the oven to 450°F to 475°F (220°C to 250°C).

Make a "double" pizza: Stretch out 1 ball of dough and place it in a well-oiled pan. Brush the top of the dough with additional oil. On a lightly floured surface, stretch out the second ball of dough and place it gently on top of the first.

Bake the pizza until deep golden brown and well-risen, about 30 minutes.

Meanwhile, blanch the greens in a saucepan of boiling salted water. Drain and chop them. In a sauté pan, sauté the greens with a little oil, the garlic, and the chile.

Remove the pizza from the oven; it should easily split lengthwise. Place the cooked greens between the 2 layers of the dough.

NOTE: *In Rome there are still men and women who work as cicoriari, or chicory pickers. You can see them in the Roman countryside. They are bent over, holding bags and knives as they search intently for chicory and other wild greens to pick. If you have a hard time finding chicory, any other slightly bitter type of green, including dandelion and broccoli rabe, will work. This is a "double" pizza, suitable for sandwiches.*

Pizza with Broccoli and Cauliflower and Coppa di Testa

- 1 (12-ounce / 350-gram) ball White Pizza Dough (page 60)
- Extra-virgin olive oil to taste
- 1 small head cauliflower
- 1 small head Romanesco broccoli
- Fine sea salt to taste
- 1 fresh chile, minced
- 1 clove garlic, minced
- 10 ounces (300 grams) coppa di testa (Italian head cheese), cut into julienne
- Zest of 1 orange
- Leaves of 1 sprig rosemary, minced

Preheat the oven to 450°F to 475°F (220°C to 250°C).

Stretch out the dough and place it in a well-oiled pan.

Bake the pizza until deep golden brown and well-risen, about 30 minutes.

While the pizza is baking, break the cauliflower and broccoli into florets and blanch them in boiling salted water; as soon as they are tender, drain. Set aside a few broccoli florets and mash the remaining broccoli and cauliflower with a fork. In a large sauté pan, sauté the broccoli and cauliflower in a small amount of oil with the chile and garlic over medium heat until slightly browned.

Remove the pizza from the oven and spread the mashed cauliflower and broccoli mixture over the surface. Scatter on the coppa pieces and sprinkle the orange zest over the surface of the pizza. Garnish with the reserved broccoli florets. Drizzle with oil and garnish with the minced rosemary. Serve piping hot.

Pizza with Romanesco Broccoli and Cured Pork Loin

- 1 pound (500 grams) Romanesco broccoli, chopped
- 1 clove garlic
- Leaves of 1 sprig rosemary
- 1 cup (250 milliliters) white wine
- Extra-virgin olive oil to taste
- Fine sea salt to taste
- 1 (12-ounce / 350-gram) ball White Pizza Dough (page 60)
- 9 ounces (250 grams) thinly sliced lonzino di maiale (cured pork loin)

Preheat the oven to 450°F to 475°F (220°C to 250°C).

In a large sauté pan, braise the broccoli in a little oil with the garlic, rosemary, and wine over medium-low heat. When the broccoli is very soft, mash it with a fork and season with salt.

Stretch out the dough and place it in a well-oiled pan.

Bake the pizza until deep golden brown and well-risen, about 30 minutes.

Remove the pizza from the oven and spread the mashed broccoli on top of the dough. Top with slices of lonzino.

Pizza with Chickpea Puree and Baccalà

- 14 ounces (400 grams) small dried chickpeas
- 1 bay leaf
- 1 clove garlic
- Leaves of 1 bunch sage
- Fine sea salt to taste
- 1 (12-ounce / 350-gram) ball White Pizza Dough (page 60)
- Extra-virgin olive oil to taste
- 1 pound (500 grams) baccalà, soaked in water to cover in the refrigerator for 1 to 3 days, with the water changed 3 times a day, then rinsed thoroughly
- Leaves of 1 sprig rosemary
- Freshly ground black pepper to taste

Soak the chickpeas overnight in water to cover. The next day, drain them and place them in a pot with water to cover, the bay leaf, garlic, and sage. Bring to a boil, then reduce the heat and simmer until the chickpeas are soft, about 45 minutes. Season with salt. Remove the bay leaf and sage, and drain off the liquid, reserving it. Process the chickpeas through a food mill, then force them through a chinois or other sieve so that you have a very creamy puree. Add a little of the reserved cooking liquid if the puree is too dry.

Preheat the oven to 450°F to 475°F (220°C to 250°C).

Stretch out the dough and place it in a well-oiled pan.

Bake the pizza until golden brown and well-risen, about 25 minutes.

While the pizza is baking, slice the baccalà very thinly.

Remove the pizza from the oven and spread the chickpea puree on top of the dough. Arrange the baccalà slices on top of the chickpeas. Drizzle with a little more oil. Sprinkle with the rosemary and season with a generous grinding of black pepper.

Pizza with Winter Vegetables or "Dry Minestrone"

- 1 (12-ounce / 350-gram) ball Mixed Grain Pizza Dough (page 62)
- Extra-virgin olive oil to taste
- 10 ounces (300 grams) boiled cranberry beans (see page 176)
- Freshly ground black pepper to taste
- 1 rib celery, diced
- 2 carrots, diced
- 2 white onions, diced
- 1 bunch kale, stemmed and chopped
- 1 clove garlic
- ½ cup (125 milliliters) vegetable broth
- Fine sea salt to taste

Preheat the oven to 450°F to 475°F (220°C to 250°C).

Stretch out the dough and place it in a well-oiled pan.

Bake the pizza until golden brown and well-risen, about 25 minutes.

While the pizza is baking, in a blender, combine the beans, 2 tablespoons oil, and a generous amount of pepper and puree. Set aside.

In a sauté pan, sauté the celery, carrots, onions, kale, and garlic in a little oil over medium heat until just beginning to brown. Remove and discard the garlic. Add the broth. Cook until the liquid has evaporated, about 10 minutes. Don't overcook; you want the vegetables to remain in distinct pieces. Season with salt and pepper.

Remove the pizza from the oven. Spread the bean puree on the surface of the dough and spoon the cooked vegetables over the puree. Drizzle with a generous amount of oil, preferably a very green and flavorful one.

Crostino with Taleggio and Cauliflower

- 1 head cauliflower
- 1 (12-ounce / 350-gram) ball White Pizza Dough (page 60)
- Extra-virgin olive oil to taste
- 2 cloves garlic, thinly sliced
- 1 dried chile, crumbled
- 9 ounces (250 grams) mozzarella cheese
- 9 ounces (250 grams) Taleggio cheese, sliced

Preheat the oven to 450°F to 475°F (220°C to 250°C).

Break the cauliflower into florets and boil in a saucepan of salted boiling water until tender. Drain the cauliflower and mash it with a fork.

Stretch out the dough and place it in a well-oiled pan. Scatter the garlic slices over the dough and sprinkle the chile over the dough. Drizzle with some oil. Break the mozzarella cheese into chunks with your hands and scatter it over the dough. Top with the mashed cauliflower and another drizzle of oil.

Bake the pizza until golden brown and well-risen, about 25 minutes.

Remove the pizza from the oven, place the Taleggio cheese slices on top, and return to the oven for an additional 5 minutes to melt the cheese. Serve hot.

Pizza with Squash, Eel, and Dandelion Greens

- 1 pound (500 grams) eel
- 1 onion, chopped
- 2 bay leaves
- Leaves of 1 bunch sage
- Leaves of 1 bunch thyme
- 1 rib celery, minced
- 1 carrot, minced
- Extra-virgin olive oil to taste
- 1 cup (250 milliliters) white wine
- 1 cup (250 milliliters) white wine vinegar
- 1 tablespoon sugar
- 2 pounds (1 kilogram) Mantovana squash or another squash with very dry flesh
- Fine sea salt to taste
- 1 (12-ounce / 350-gram) ball White Pizza Dough (page 60)
- 1 bunch dandelion greens or other bitter greens, such as arugula or chicory
- Juice of 1 lemon

Preheat the oven to 400°F (200°C).

Gut and remove the gills from the eel. Dry it thoroughly with a dish towel.

In a large pot over medium heat, brown the onion with the herbs, celery, and carrot in a small amount of oil. Add the wine, vinegar, and sugar and bring to a boil.

Reduce the heat and add the eel. Simmer until cooked, about 20 minutes. Let the eel cool in the liquid.

Meanwhile, seed the squash and cut it onto thick slices. Line a baking sheet with parchment paper and arrange the squash slices on it in a single layer. Bake until soft, about 25 minutes. Scoop out the cooked squash flesh with a spoon. Puree the squash in a blender with a drizzle of oil and a pinch of salt.

Raise the oven temperature to 450°F to 475°F (220°C to 250°C).

Stretch out the dough and place it in a well-oiled pan. Bake until golden brown and well-risen, about 25 minutes.

While the pizza is baking, remove the eel from the liquid. Bone the eel and cut it into small pieces. Tear the dandelion greens into small pieces and toss them in a bowl with the lemon juice, some oil, and a small amount of salt.

Remove the pizza from the oven and spread the squash puree on the surface. Scatter the dandelion greens on top and arrange the eel pieces over the greens in a single layer.

Pizza with Sardinian Artichokes

- 10 Sardinian artichokes or other small artichokes
- Juice of 1 lemon
- Extra-virgin olive oil to taste
- Fine sea salt to taste
- Freshly ground black pepper to taste
- 1 (12-ounce / 350-gram) ball White Pizza Dough (page 60)

Preheat the oven to 400°F (200°F).

Trim the artichokes, removing any hard external leaves. Halve the artichokes and scrape out the hairy chokes. Fill a bowl with cold water and the lemon juice. Thinly slice the artichokes and drop them into the acidulated water for a few minutes.

Meanwhile, line a pan with parchment paper. (A round pan is fine.) Remove the artichoke slices from the water, toss them with oil, and season with salt and pepper. Spread the artichokes in a single layer on the lined pan. Stretch out the dough and rest it on top of the artichokes.

Bake the pizza until deep golden brown and well-risen, about 30 minutes.

Before serving, invert the pan so the dough is on the bottom. Lift off the pan, peel off the parchment paper, and serve hot.

Pizza with Curly Puntarelle

- 10 ounces (300 grams) puntarelle greens
- 1 (12-ounce / 350-gram) ball White Pizza Dough (page 60)
- Extra-virgin olive oil to taste
- 1 salted anchovy, rinsed, boned, and chopped
- ½ clove garlic, crushed
- 10 ounces (300 grams) sun-dried tomatoes in oil
- 2 large hard-boiled eggs

Preheat the oven to 450°F to 475°F (220°C to 250°C).

PREPARE THE PUNTARELLE: Set up a bowl of ice water. Wash the leaves and cut them lengthwise into thin strips. Transfer the strips to the ice water, where they will curl up.

Stretch out the dough and place it in a well-oiled pan. Bake the pizza until golden brown and well-risen, about 25 minutes.

While the pizza is baking, prepare the dressing for the puntarelle by grinding together (a mortar and pestle works well) the anchovy, some oil, and the garlic.

Drain the sun-dried tomatoes, mince with a mezzaluna, and set aside. Finely mince 1 egg and dice the other egg into larger pieces. Set aside.

Remove the puntarelle from the ice water, pat dry, and toss with the dressing.

Remove the pizza from the oven. Spread the minced sun-dried tomatoes on the surface of the dough and top with the dressed puntarelle. Sprinkle the hard-boiled eggs over the puntarelle.

Puntarelle are Rome's most famous greens. They are a kind of chicory, similar to dandelion greens, and are always served with an anchovy dressing.

Pizza Stuffed with Mortadella, Puntarelle, and Anchovies

- 2 (12-ounce / 350-gram) balls White Pizza Dough (page 60)
- Extra-virgin olive oil to taste
- 9 ounces (250 grams) puntarelle greens (see page 195)
- 3½ ounces (100 grams) anchovies in oil (see Note)
- 10 ounces (300 grams) sliced mortadella

Preheat the oven to 450°F to 475°F (220°C to 250°C).

MAKE A "DOUBLE" PIZZA: Stretch out 1 ball of dough and place it in a well-oiled pan. Brush the top of the dough with additional oil. On a lightly floured surface, stretch out the second ball of dough and place it gently on top of the first.

Bake the pizza until deep golden brown and well-risen, about 30 minutes.

While the pizza is baking, prepare the puntarelle: Set up a bowl of ice water. Wash the leaves and cut them lengthwise into thin strips. Transfer the strips to the ice water, where they will curl up.

Remove the pizza from the oven; it should pull apart easily. Remove the anchovies from the oil and place them between the layers. Insert the puntarelle and mortadella between the layers as well. Serve at room temperature.

To make anchovies in oil, at least 2 days before you plan to make the pizza, combine 1 cup (250 milliliters) vinegar with 1 cup (250 milliliters) water in a bowl. Bone salted anchovies and rinse the fillets in the vinegar mixture, then transfer them to a nonreactive container. Add enough oil to cover the anchovies. Refrigerate for 48 hours before using.

Pizza with Four Cheeses

- 1 (12-ounce / 350-gram) ball White Pizza Dough (page 60)
- Extra-virgin olive oil to taste
- 5 ounces (150 grams) stracchino, diced
- 5 ounces (150 grams) Gorgonzola, diced
- 5 ounces (150 grams) pecorino Romano, diced
- 5 ounces (150 grams) Fontina, diced

Preheat the oven to 450°F to 475°F (220°C to 250°C).

Stretch out the dough and place it in a well-oiled pan. Bake for 10 minutes.

Remove the pizza from the oven and scatter the cheeses over the surface. Bake for an additional 15 minutes, until golden brown, and serve hot.

You can use any combination of cheeses you like, but do aim for a mix of hard and soft types.

Amatriciana-style Pizza

- 1¼ cups (300 grams) canned peeled tomatoes
- Extra-virgin olive oil to taste
- Fine sea salt to taste
- 1 (12-ounce / 350-gram) ball White Pizza Dough (page 60)
- 10 ounces (300 grams) guanciale (see Note), diced
- 7 ounces (200 grams) grated pecorino Romano
- Freshly ground black pepper to taste

Preheat the oven to 450˚F to 475˚F (220˚C to 250˚C).

Crush the tomatoes with your hands into a small bowl. Drizzle with some oil, season lightly with salt, and toss to combine.

Stretch out the dough and place it in a well-oiled pan. Spread the tomato mixture on top and scatter on the guanciale.

Bake until golden brown and well-risen, about 25 minutes.

Remove the pizza from the oven. Sprinkle the grated cheeses over top and season with a generous amount of pepper. Serve immediately.

NOTE: *Guanciale is cured pork jowl. Pancetta makes an acceptable substitute.*

Pizza with Duck and Oranges

- 6 oranges
- 1 14-ounce (400-gram) duck breast
- 2 tablespoons (20 grams) sugar
- Leaves of 1 sprig thyme
- Fine sea salt to taste
- Freshly ground black pepper to taste
- 1 cup (250 milliliters) dry white wine
- 1 (12-ounce / 350-gram) ball Mixed Grain Pizza Dough (page 62)
- Extra-virgin olive oil to taste
- 10 black olives, pitted
- 2 to 3 mint leaves

Preheat the oven to 450°F to 475°F (220°C to 250°C).

Juice 3 of the oranges. Heat a sauté pan over very high heat and place the duck breast in it with the skin side down. Brown for 5 minutes. Spoon off any rendered fat and transfer it to a small saucepan. Return the pan with the duck breast to the heat. Set aside 1 tablespoon of orange juice and add the rest to the duck fat, along with the sugar and thyme leaves; season with salt and pepper. Place over medium heat and cook until reduced to a thick sauce.

Meanwhile, continue cooking the duck; when it is nicely browned on all sides, add the wine and cook until the wine has evaporated. Brush the orange sauce onto the duck. Keep the duck warm until you're ready to serve the pizza.

Use a mandoline to slice 2 oranges (including the peel) very thinly. Stretch the dough and place it in a well-oiled pan. Scatter the sliced oranges on top of the dough in a single layer and bake the pizza until golden brown and well-risen, about 25 minutes.

Cut the duck breast into ½- to ¾-inch (1- to 2-centimeter) slices. Section the remaining orange (discard the peel, pith, and membrane) and toss it with the olives. Whisk together about 1 tablespoon oil and the reserved tablespoon of orange juice and toss to combine with the olives and orange segments.

Remove the pizza from the oven and top with the duck breast slices. Scatter the olives and orange sections on top and drizzle with any juices left in the bowl. Tear the mint leaves and scatter them over the pizza. Serve piping hot.

Pizza with Spinach, Conciato di San Vittore, and Guanciale

- 1 bunch spinach
- Extra-virgin olive oil to taste
- Fine sea salt to taste
- Freshly ground black pepper to taste
- 1 (12-ounce / 350-gram) ball White Pizza Dough (page 60)
- 10 ounces (300 grams) Conciato di San Vittore (see Notes) or other sheep's-milk cheese, sliced
- 20 slices guanciale cotto al vino (see Notes) or plain guanciale

Preheat the oven to 450°F to 475°F (220°C to 250°C).

Rinse the spinach in several changes of water, then cook it briefly in a saucepan with the water that remains on the leaves. Squeeze dry and season with a drizzle of oil and some salt and pepper.

Stretch out the dough and place it in a well-oiled pan.

Bake until golden brown and well-risen, about 25 minutes.

Remove the pizza from the oven. Arrange the cheese on top in a single layer, then the spinach, and the guanciale last. Return the pizza to the oven for a few minutes to melt the cheese, then serve immediately.

NOTE: *Conciato di San Vittore cheese has a long history in the Lazio region, but it is not very well-known these days. My friend cheesemaker Vincenzo Mancini is bringing this sheep's-milk cheese back into the spotlight with a very high-quality version.* Conciato *means "cured," and in this case the cheese is cured with spices on the crust: juniper berries, bay leaf, wild thyme, wild fennel, coriander, sage, black and white pepper, basil, rosemary, and anise.*

Guanciale cotto al vino is a pig jowl that is cooked in wine from Cori, a town in Lazio not far from Latina, before it is cured. It is particularly tender and aromatic.

Pizza with Fennel, Salmon, and Treviso Radicchio

- 3 bulbs fennel
- 1 head Treviso radicchio
- 10 ounces (300 grams) smoked salmon (see Note)
- 1 (12-ounce / 350-gram) ball White Pizza Dough (page 60)
- Extra-virgin olive oil to taste
- 7 ounces (200 grams) grated grana cheese

Preheat the oven to 450°F to 475°F (220°C to 250°C).

Cut the fennel into thin slices. Cut the radicchio lengthwise and grill or broil it, turning, until lightly charred. Thinly slice the smoked salmon and set aside.

Stretch out the dough and place it in a well-oiled pan. Scatter the fennel slices on top.

Bake the pizza for 25 minutes, then sprinkle the grated cheese on top and return to the oven for 5 minutes. If the cheese hasn't browned, broil the pizza briefly.

Remove the pizza from the oven. Cut it into equal-size squares and make sandwiches with the salmon and the grilled radicchio. Serve at room temperature.

Use wild salmon if at all possible. It's better to slice it yourself when you're ready to use it rather than buying precut salmon.

Pizza with Leeks, Gruyère, and Lots of Nutmeg

- Extra-virgin olive oil to taste
- 4 leeks (see Notes), thinly sliced
- 1 (12-ounce / 350-gram) ball White Pizza Dough (page 60)
- 9 ounces (250 grams) Gruyère, thinly sliced
- Grated nutmeg to taste (see Notes)

Preheat the oven to 450°F to 475°F (220°C to 250°C).

Place a small amount of oil in a pan over medium heat and sauté the leeks until wilted. Add ½ cup (125 milliliters) water and braise the leeks until they are soft and most of the water has evaporated.

Stretch out the dough and place it in a well-oiled pan.

Bake the pizza until golden brown and well-risen, about 25 minutes.

Remove the pizza from the oven and spread the cooked leeks on top of the dough. Arrange the cheese on top of the leeks. Grate on a generous amount of nutmeg. Serve hot.

Aim for a light, even dusting of nutmeg—too much will cover up the other flavors. Look for small leeks, as the larger ones tend to be tough.

Pizza with Cabbage and Pork

- 2 (12-ounce / 350-gram) balls Mixed Grain Pizza Dough (page 62)
- Extra-virgin olive oil to taste
- 1 head Savoy cabbage (see Note), thinly sliced
- 1 unpeeled clove garlic
- 1 chile, seeded
- ½ cup dry white wine
- 10 ounces (300 grams) roast pork (see page 101), sliced
- 1 tablespoon honey

Preheat the oven to 450°F to 475°F (220°C to 250°C).

Make a "double" pizza: Stretch out 1 ball of dough and place it in a well-oiled pan. Brush the top of the dough with additional oil. On a lightly floured surface, stretch out the second ball of dough and place it gently on top of the first.

Bake the pizza until golden brown and well-risen, about 25 minutes.

Meanwhile, heat a small amount of oil in a large sauté pan. Add the cabbage, garlic, and chile. Sauté until the cabbage is wilted, 2 to 3 minutes, then add the wine and cook until the cabbage is tender and the liquid has evaporated. Remove and discard the garlic and chile.

Remove the pizza from the oven and separate the 2 layers. Distribute the cabbage on the bottom layer. Arrange the pork slices in a single layer on top of the cabbage. Drizzle with a little oil and the honey. Top with the top layer of the pizza and cut into sandwiches. Serve hot.

Savoy cabbage is more tender and delicately flavored than regular green cabbage.

Cardoon Pizza

- 4 tablespoons (50 grams) unsalted butter
- 1 bunch cardoons (see Note), trimmed and peeled
- ¾ cup (200 milliliters) heavy cream
- Grated nutmeg to taste
- 3½ ounces (100 grams) grated grana cheese
- 1 (12-ounce / 350-gram) ball White Pizza Dough (page 60)
- Extra-virgin olive oil to taste

Preheat the oven to 350°F (180°C).

Butter a baking sheet and place the cardoons on it. Add the cream, some nutmeg, and the grana. Bake for 15 minutes, until tender. Remove from the oven and set aside on the baking sheet.

Raise the oven temperature to 450°F to 475°F (220°C to 250°C).

Stretch out the dough and place it in a well-oiled pan.

Bake the pizza until golden brown and well-risen, about 25 minutes.

Remove the pizza from the oven, turn on the broiler, and broil the cardoons for 5 minutes to brown them. Place the cardoons on top of the pizza. Serve on dishes with silverware; this pizza is a little too messy to eat out of hand.

NOTE: *Cardoon is a large and beautiful plant related to the artichoke. Its stalks, which resemble those of celery, are prized for their unusual taste.*

LSD (Licorice, Sausage, and Date) Pizza

- 1 (12-ounce / 350-gram) ball White Pizza Dough (page 60)
- Extra-virgin olive oil to taste
- 7 ounces (200 grams) dried dates, pitted
- 5 pure licorice candies
- 2 spicy cured pork sausages
- 10 fresh dates (see Note), pitted and sliced

Preheat the oven to 450°F to 475°F (220°C to 250°C).

Stretch out the dough and place it in a well-oiled pan.

Bake the pizza until golden brown and well-risen, about 25 minutes.

While the pizza is baking, puree the dried dates in a food processor until smooth. Crush the licorice candies in a mortar and pestle and break up the sausages with your hands.

Remove the pizza from the oven. Spread the date puree on the dough and scatter the pieces of sausage on top of it. Sprinkle with a little licorice powder (taste and decide how much to use). Top with the fresh date slices.

I like the special aroma and flavor of fresh dates, but you can use dried dates if you don't care for fresh dates or they aren't available.

SPRING PIZZAS

Pizza with Squash Blossoms, Mozzarella, and Anchovies

- 4 zucchini
- 1 (12-ounce / 350-gram) ball White Pizza Dough (page 60)
- Extra-virgin olive oil to taste
- 9 ounces (250 grams) buffalo mozzarella
- 10 squash blossoms
- 10 Cantábrico salted anchovies (see Note), rinsed and boned

Preheat the oven to 450˚F to 475˚F (220˚C to 250˚C).

Slice the zucchini into thin rounds.

Stretch out the dough and place it in a well-oiled pan. Arrange the zucchini slices on the dough.

Bake the pizza until golden brown and well-risen, about 25 minutes.

Remove the pizza from the oven. Break up the mozzarella by hand and place it on top of the zucchini. Arrange the squash blossoms among the mozzarella, and place the anchovies on top. Serve hot. (You can also cut the pizza into squares and arrange them as sandwiches, as shown in the photo.)

For this recipe I call for Spanish Cantábrico anchovies because I find them very delicate; they won't overwhelm the subtle flavor of the squash blossoms.

Pizza with Asparagus, Pancetta, Parmigiano, and Lemon

- 1 pound (500 grams) asparagus
- Fine sea salt to taste
- 1 white onion, thinly sliced
- Extra-virgin olive oil to taste
- 5 ounces (150 grams) grated Parmigiano-Reggiano
- 1 lemon
- 1 (12-ounce / 350-gram) ball White Pizza Dough (page 60)
- 7 ounces (200 grams) sliced rolled pancetta

Preheat the oven to 450°F to 475°F (220°C to 250°C).

Cut off the tips of the asparagus spears. Blanch them in a saucepan of boiling salted water until just tender, then remove with a slotted spoon and transfer to a bowl of ice water to stop the cooking. Reserve the cooking water.

Chop the remaining portions of the asparagus. In a sauté pan, sauté the onion in a little oil over medium heat until translucent, then add the asparagus stalks. Add 1 cup (250 milliliters) of the asparagus cooking water and simmer briskly until tender, about 15 minutes. Transfer the stalks to a blender (an immersion blender also works well). Add about ¼ cup (40 grams) of the grated cheese and the juice of half the lemon and blend until smooth.

Stretch out the dough and place it in a well-oiled pan. Spread the asparagus puree on top of the dough. Bake the pizza for 10 minutes.

Remove the pizza from the oven, arrange the pancetta on top in a single layer, and return to the oven for an additional 15 minutes, until golden brown. Scatter on the cooked asparagus tips. Zest the lemon over the pizza and sprinkle with the remaining grated cheese.

Onion Pizza

- 1 pound (500 grams) yellow onions (see Note)
- Extra-virgin olive oil to taste
- Fine sea salt to taste
- Freshly ground black pepper to taste
- 1 (12-ounce / 350-gram) ball White Pizza Dough (page 60)

Preheat the oven to 450°F to 475°F (220°C to 250°C).

Thinly slice the onions. Place them in a large bowl and toss with a generous amount of oil. Season with salt and pepper. Stretch out the dough and place it in a well-oiled pan. Distribute the onions on the pizza dough.

Bake the pizza until deep golden brown and well-risen, about 30 minutes.

Remove the pizza from the oven and serve warm or cold.

NOTE: *If you prefer a milder onion flavor, rinse the onions in milk after slicing them, then rinse them with water, dry them carefully, and place them on the pizza dough.*

Pizza with Roman-style Tripe

- 1 rib celery, minced
- 2 carrots, minced
- 1 onion, minced
- 1 clove garlic
- Extra-virgin olive oil to taste
- 1 pound (500 grams) tripe, cleaned and cut into strips
- 1 cup (250 milliliters) white wine
- Fine sea salt to taste
- Freshly ground black pepper to taste
- 1 cup (250 grams) tomato puree
- 1 (12-ounce / 350-gram) ball White Pizza Dough (page 60)
- 1 cup (250 grams) canned peeled tomatoes
- 5 ounces (150 grams) grated pecorino Romano
- 6 to 8 leaves mint

In a sauté pan over medium heat, sauté the celery, carrots, onion, and garlic in a small amount of oil.

When the onion is golden, add the tripe. (In Rome we like our tripe thick and in pieces that are on the large side.) Brown the tripe, and then add the wine. Turn the heat to high and let the liquid evaporate. Season with salt and pepper and add the tomato puree. Reduce the heat to low and cook until the tripe is tender, at least 25 minutes.

While the tripe is cooking, preheat the oven to 450°F to 475°F (220°C to 250°C).

Stretch out the dough and place it in a well-oiled pan. Crush the peeled tomatoes by hand into a small bowl. Season with salt and pepper and stir in a little oil. Spread the tomato mixture on the surface of the dough.

Bake the pizza until golden brown and well-risen, about 25 minutes.

Remove the pizza from the oven and distribute the tripe on top. Sprinkle with the cheese and mint. Add a generous grinding of black pepper and serve hot.

Spring Vegetable Pizza

- 4 spring onions
- 9 ounces (250 grams) young fava beans
- 9 ounces (250 grams) fresh shell peas
- 4 artichokes
- 5 ounces (150 grams) guanciale, diced
- 1 cup white wine
- 1 (12-ounce / 350-gram) ball White Pizza Dough (page 60)
- 10 ounces (300 grams) yellow potatoes, such as Yukon golds, boiled and peeled
- 5 ounces (150 grams) grated pecorino Romano

Preheat the oven to 450°F to 475°F (220°C to 250°C).

Thinly slice the spring onions and shell the fava beans. (Young fava beans won't have the hard skin around each bean, but if the beans are not perfectly young and do have that skin, remove it.) Shell the peas. Trim the artichokes, removing any hard outer leaves and the hairy choke. Thinly slice the artichokes. Heat a sauté pan and cook the guanciale until it releases some of its fat. Add the spring onions, fava beans, peas, and artichokes to the pan. Add the wine and cook until the liquid has evaporated and the vegetables are tender.

Stretch out the dough and place it in a well-oiled pan. Break the potatoes into pieces and distribute them on top of the dough.

Bake the pizza until deep golden brown and well-risen, about 30 minutes.

Remove the pizza from the oven and spread the cooked vegetables and guanciale over the potatoes. Sprinkle with the cheese and serve hot.

All About Artichokes Pizza

- 12 Roman artichokes or other baby artichokes
- Juice of 1 lemon
- Extra-virgin olive oil to taste
- 2 cloves garlic
- 1 chile
- Leaves of 1 bunch flat-leaf parsley, minced
- 4 to 5 leaves mint, minced
- 1 cup (250 milliliters) dry white wine
- Fine sea salt to taste
- 1 (12-ounce / 350-gram) ball Mixed Grain Pizza Dough (page 62)

Preheat the oven to 450˚F to 475˚F (220˚C to 250˚C).

Trim the artichokes, removing any hard outer leaves and the hairy choke. Fill a bowl with cold water and add the lemon juice. Drop the artichokes into the acidulated water for a few minutes.

Prepare the artichokes four different ways: Cut 5 of the artichokes in half and return them to the acidulated water. Cut 3 of the artichokes into thicker slices and sauté in a sauté pan in a small amount of oil with the garlic, chile, parsley, and mint. Add the white wine and cook until the liquid has evaporated. Boil 4 artichokes in salted water; as soon as they are tender, remove them with a slotted spoon and puree them in a blender. Force the artichoke puree through a sieve to create a perfectly smooth puree. Emulsify the puree with a little oil until thickened and set aside. Remove 3 artichokes from the acidulated water. Thinly slice them, dry them thoroughly, and fry them in a generous amount of oil until the edges are brown and crispy. Thinly slice the remaining 2 artichokes and leave them raw.

Stretch out the dough and place it in a well-oiled pan.

Bake until golden brown and well-risen, about 25 minutes.

Remove the pizza from the oven. Spread the artichoke puree on the dough and scatter the sautéed artichokes on top of the puree. Place the fried artichokes on top of the sautéed artichokes and top with the raw artichokes.

recipes / **spring**

Pizza with Eggs, Asparagus, and Lemon

- 1 bunch asparagus
- Fine sea salt to taste
- Extra-virgin olive oil to taste
- Juice of 1 lemon
- 1 (12-ounce / 350-gram) ball Mixed Grain Pizza Dough (page 62)
- 4 large eggs
- Freshly ground black pepper to taste

Preheat the oven to 450°F to 475°F (220°C to 250°C).

Blanch the asparagus in a saucepan of boiling salted water for 3 minutes, until barely tender but not mushy. Remove with a slotted spoon.

Leave the tips intact and slice the stalks into thin rounds. In a sauté pan, sauté the asparagus with a tablespoon or so of oil and the lemon juice.

Stretch out the dough and place it in a well-oiled pan.

Bake the pizza until golden brown and well-risen, about 25 minutes.

While the pizza is baking, prepare the eggs: Heat a tablespoon or so of oil in a skillet and add the eggs. As soon as they begin to sizzle, beat them with a wooden spoon.

Remove the pizza from the oven. Spread the scrambled eggs on top of the dough and top the eggs with the asparagus. Season with salt and pepper and serve immediately.

Pizza with Coffee-flavored Lamb and Snow Peas

- 1 boneless leg of lamb
- 4 boneless lamb ribs
- Fine sea salt, preferably fleur de sel (see Note), to taste
- Freshly ground black pepper
- 3 cloves garlic, minced
- Leaves of 1 sprig rosemary, minced
- ⅛ cup (100 milliliters) brewed espresso
- 1 (12-ounce / 350-gram) ball Mixed Grain Pizza Dough (page 62)
- Extra-virgin olive oil to taste
- 1 pound (500 grams) snow peas

Preheat the oven to 400°F (200°C). Rub the lamb leg and ribs with salt, pepper, the garlic, and the rosemary and set aside while the oven is preheating.

Roast the lamb for 40 minutes, until it is crisp on the outside but still fairly rare. Splash on the espresso and return to the oven for 5 minutes more. Remove and reserve both the lamb and coffee-flavored juices.

Raise the oven temperature to 450°F to 475°F (220°C to 250°C).

Stretch out the dough and place it in a well-oiled pan.

Bake the pizza until golden brown and well-risen, about 25 minutes.

While the pizza is baking, blanch the snow peas in a saucepan of salted boiling water. Drain and chop the snow peas. Slice the lamb.

Remove the pizza from the oven. Arrange slices of lamb on the dough and scatter on the chopped snow peas. Drizzle with the lamb juices and sprinkle with a little fleur de sel.

Fleur de sel is a flaky sea salt. It provides a touch of crunch and contrasts with the silky texture of the lamb.

Calzone with Endive, Olives, and Anchovies

- 1 (12-ounce / 350-gram) ball Mixed Grain Pizza Dough (page 62)
- 1 head curly endive or escarole
- 5 salted anchovies, rinsed and boned
- 20 black olives, preferably Gaeta, pitted
- Extra-virgin olive oil to taste
- Fine sea salt to taste
- Freshly ground black pepper to taste

Preheat the oven to 450°F to 475°F (220°C to 250°C).

Stretch the dough into a circle and arrange it on a baking pan. Place the whole head of endive or escarole, the anchovies, and the olives in the center of the circle of dough. Drizzle with some oil and season with salt and pepper. (Keep in mind that the olives and the anchovies are salty.)

Fold the dough in half to form a semicircle. Pinch the edges together to seal.

Bake the calzone until golden brown, about 25 minutes. Serve piping hot.

Pizza with Buffalo Mozzarella and Bitter Greens

- 10 ounces (300 grams) chicory
- 1 bunch dandelion greens
- 1 bunch arugula
- Extra-virgin olive oil to taste
- Fine sea salt to taste
- Freshly ground black pepper to taste
- 1 cup (250 grams) canned peeled tomatoes
- 1 (12-ounce / 350-gram) ball White Pizza Dough (page 60)
- 9 ounces (250 grams) buffalo mozzarella, sliced

Preheat the oven to 450°F to 475°F (220°C to 250°C).

Mince the chicory, dandelion greens, and arugula and toss with some oil, salt, and pepper. Set aside.

Crush the tomatoes through your fingers into a small bowl. Toss with a little oil and some salt.

Stretch out the dough and place it in a well-oiled pan. Distribute the tomato mixture on top of the dough.

Bake the pizza until golden brown and well-risen, about 25 minutes.

Remove the pizza from the oven and immediately layer the cheese slices on top. Scatter the minced greens over the cheese.

Pizza with Tuna-style Chicken

- 1 free-range chicken, skinned and boned
- Zest and juice of 1 lemon
- Leaves of 1 sprig thyme
- 1 bay leaf
- 2 whole cloves
- 1 quart (1 liter) extra-virgin olive oil, plus more to taste
- 2 green tomatoes
- 1 (12-ounce / 350-gram) ball Mixed Grain Pizza Dough (page 62)
- Fine sea salt to taste
- 1 head curly endive

Preheat the oven to 450°F to 475°F (220°C to 250°C).

Chop the chicken into bite-size pieces and place them in 2 glass jars with the zest of the lemon, the thyme leaves, bay leaf, and cloves divided between the jars. Fill the jars with the oil to cover the chicken completely. (If not, add a little more until the chicken is covered.) Tightly screw the lids on the jars. Fill a large stockpot with water and bring to a simmer over medium heat. Carefully place the jars in the pot, making sure they are fully submerged. Cook the jars for 20 minutes at a gentle simmer. Let the jars cool slightly before opening. The results should be similar to tuna canned in oil. If you are not eating all of the chicken the same day, pour the contents of the jars into a fresh container and store in the refrigerator.

Thinly slice the green tomatoes. Stretch out the dough and place it in a well-oiled pan. Place the green tomato slices on top in a single layer. Drizzle with a generous amount of oil and season with salt.

Bake the pizza until golden brown and well-risen, about 25 minutes.

Remove the pizza from the oven and let it rest at room temperature for 10 minutes.

Meanwhile, tear the endive into pieces and in a bowl, dress it with the lemon juice and some oil.

Arrange the chicken pieces on top of the tomatoes, scatter the dressed endive on top of the chicken, and serve.

Pizza with Fava Beans and Pecorino

- 10 ounces (300 grams) fava beans
- 1 (12-ounce / 350-gram) ball White Pizza Dough (page 60)
- Extra-virgin olive oil to taste
- 10 ounces (300 grams) mozzarella, sliced
- 9 ounces (250 grams) soft (not aged) sheep's-milk cheese (fresh pecorino) or caciotta, sliced

Preheat the oven to 450°F to 475°F (220°C to 250°C).

Shell and skin the fava beans.

Stretch out the dough and place it in a well-oiled pan. Place the mozzarella cheese slices on the surface in a single layer and scatter on the fava beans.

Bake the pizza until golden brown and well-risen, about 25 minutes.

Remove the pizza from the oven and immediately arrange the sheep's-milk cheese slices on top. Set aside for a minute or two to allow the cheese to melt, then serve.

Pizza with Edible Flowers

- 10 ounces (300 grams) puntarelle (see Note, page 195)
- 1 (12-ounce / 350-gram) ball White Pizza Dough (page 60)
- Extra-virgin olive oil to taste
- 1¼ cups (300 grams) canned peeled tomatoes
- Fine sea salt to taste
- 9 ounces (250 grams) mozzarella
- 4 piquillo peppers (see Note)
- Edible flowers, such as daisies, roses, violets, and chrysanthemums

Preheat the oven to 450°F to 475°F (220°C to 250°C).

PREPARE THE PUNTARELLE: Set up a bowl of ice water. Wash the leaves and cut them lengthwise in thin strips. Transfer the strips to the ice water, where they will curl up.

Stretch out the dough and place it in a well-oiled pan. Distribute the tomatoes on top of the dough, crushing them with your hands.

Bake the pizza until golden brown and well-risen, about 25 minutes.

Remove the pizza from the oven. Drizzle with a little oil and season with salt. Set aside to cool to room temperature.

Arrange the cheese, peppers, and flowers on top of the pizza. You can do this any way that you wish: Slice the mozzarella, or try dicing it and creating a checkerboard pattern with squares of diced mozzarella and squares of flowers.

NOTE: *Piquillo peppers are Spanish pickled peppers that have been peeled and lightly charred. They have an incredible flavor and a firm texture.*

Pizza with Friggitelli Peppers and Baccalà

- 1 (12-ounce / 350-gram) ball White Pizza Dough (page 60)
- Extra-virgin olive oil to taste
- 10 ounces (300 grams) friggitelli peppers (see Note)
- 1 clove garlic, minced
- 1 chile, minced
- 1 pound (500 grams) baccalà, soaked in water to cover in the refrigerator for 1 to 3 days, with the water changed 3 times a day, then rinsed thoroughly
- Freshly ground black pepper to taste
- Zest of 1 lemon

Preheat the oven to 450°F to 475°F (220°C to 250°C).

Stretch out the dough and place it in a well-oiled pan.

Bake the pizza until golden brown and well-risen, about 25 minutes.

Meanwhile, chop the peppers. Heat a sauté pan until very hot; add a small amount of oil and sauté the peppers with the garlic and chile until softened and slightly browned on the edges.

Thinly slice the baccalà as if making carpaccio.

Remove the pizza from the oven and spread the peppers on top of the dough. Arrange the baccalà slices on top. Season with a generous amount of pepper and sprinkle with the lemon zest.

Friggitelli peppers are a variety grown in Lazio. They are sweet peppers with a fairly chewy texture and not much flesh. Their flavor is intense.

Fried Pizza

- 1¼ cups (300 grams) tomato puree
- Extra-virgin olive oil to taste
- Fine sea salt to taste
- Peanut oil for frying
- 1 (12-ounce / 350-gram) ball White Pizza Dough (page 60)
- 10 ounces (300 grams) mozzarella, cut into 10 pieces
- 7 ounces (200 grams) grated grana cheese
- 10 young basil leaves

Mix the tomato puree with some oil and salt and set aside.

Heat peanut oil for frying to 350° F (175° C) in a large pot or in a deep fryer.

Cut the dough into 10 walnut-size pieces. Fry the pieces of dough in the oil until they are crisp and golden, then remove them with a strainer and set them on paper towels or brown paper bags to drain.

Top each fried piece of dough with a little of the tomato sauce, a piece of mozzarella cheese, a sprinkling of grana cheese, and a basil leaf. Serve very hot.

Pizza Struffoli

- Peanut oil for frying
- 1 (12-ounce / 350-gram) ball White Pizza Dough (page 60)
- ½ cup (150 grams) honey
- Sugar confetti or other decorations

Heat peanut oil for frying to 350° F (175° C) in a large pot or in a deep fryer.

Cut the dough into little sticks. (Slightly irregular size and shape is fine.) Fry the pieces of dough until golden, 3 to 4 minutes. Remove them with a strainer and set them on paper towels or brown paper bags to drain.

Place the honey in a small saucepan and warm it over medium heat until it is very liquid. Drizzle the honey all over the struffoli. Garnish with the sugar confetti.

Struffoli are little fried pastries that kids eat during Carnival.

In the Kitchen at Pizzarium

Federico

Tommaso and Gabriele

Matteo

Shankir

251

A Note from the Translator

There is no one-to-one correspondence between the flours sold in Italy and the flours sold in the United States. Even figuring out the equivalent protein content is difficult, as two different systems are used. (In Italy flours are given a W number, while in the United States we talk about percentages.) In both countries, many manufacturers don't provide a figure at all, either because the protein content of their flours varies too widely or because they haven't bothered to figure out what it is.

I have tried the dough recipes in this book with several different types of flour, and only one was not appropriate: Do not use all-purpose flour in these recipes. The flavor was fine, but the flour doesn't develop enough gluten, so attempting to stretch the dough was frustrating. Even after a long resting period, it kept snapping back and tearing.

For his White Pizza Dough (page 60), Gabriele calls for type 0 flour. While Italian type 00 flour and some facsimiles of it are available in the United States, I have never seen type 0 flour on the shelves, so I replaced it with bread flour, which works beautifully.

Two of the recipes also call for Buratto flour, which is milled by Mulino Marino (www.mulinomarino.it) from a special strain of wheat. Buratto flour has about 13% protein and is a high-extraction flour (see Gabriele's discussion on page 28). Burrato flour is available in the United States at Williams-Sonoma (www.williams-sonoma.com) and in some other specialty stores. It's pricey but worth it. The dough I made with Buratto was significantly better.

If you absolutely cannot locate it, seek out high-extraction flour as a replacement. King Arthur sells one (labeled First Clear Flour), as do Heartland Mill (www.heartlandmill.com), Bay State Milling (www.baystatemilling.com), and many other mills. Or, seek out locally milled flour for the freshest product. You can also make your own high-extraction flour—simply strain whole wheat flour through a sieve to remove the bran and germ.

Farro and spelt are slightly different grains, both very ancient types of wheat. If you were to cook whole farro (often used in soups and salads) and whole spelt side-by-side, you would note the difference, both visually and in the way the grains cook and taste. That said, flours made with spelt and flours made with farro are not that different. Farro flour is available in the United States, and if you can find it, use it. Mulino Marino's farro flour (confusingly labeled as spelt flour in English) is sold at Williams-Sonoma alongside Buratto flour. Bluebird Grain Farms (bluebirdgrainfarms.com) makes farro flour, and imported Italian farro flour can be purchased at many specialty shops, such as Formaggio Kitchen (www.formaggiokitchen.com).

However, the only farro flour I have ever found for sale is whole-grain (integrale) farro flour. In the Mixed Grain pizza dough (page 62), Gabriele calls for both light farro flour and whole-grain farro flour. While my search for a light farro flour went unrewarded, Bob's Red Mill (www.bobsredmill.com) makes both light and whole-grain spelt flour, which can be ordered online. I made the Mixed Grain Pizza Dough with the Bob's Red Mill flours, and it worked just as well.

A word about water: I consistently used much more water than each recipe's listed amount, which appears to be a baseline. The dough should be fairly soft (but not runny). It will firm up dramatically during the folding stage. Use the photographs as a guide. When it comes to "wet" toppings—such as zucchini or eggplant—try to seek out varieties with a low water content to prevent sogginess.

The rising times are also guidelines, and you have a great deal of leeway. The dough is time-intensive, as it does need some time to rise, but it's really not labor-intensive, and the process is very flexible. Putting the dough in the refrigerator retards rising and develops a terrific flavor, but if you are in a hurry you can let your dough rise at room temperature and bake it the same day. And if something comes up and you can't bake the pizza when you intended to, it will last a little longer in the refrigerator, too, especially if you used a natural yeast starter.

And speaking of natural yeast starters, don't be intimidated! Getting one up and running is not difficult, and they are not as high-maintenance as they sound. When I started testing these recipes, I had a starter in my own refrigerator that had been unused for more than a year. I brought the jar of starter to room temperature, refreshed it twice a day, and in less than a week it was bubbling and active again. Also, keep in mind that dough may not rise dramatically when made with natural yeast. Many starters instead give great "oven spring" to breads as they bake. As you work with your starter, you will develop a feel for it and get to know what to expect. It will be as individual as a fingerprint.

Gabriele's recipes make a lot of dough. One batch will make enough for six medium pizzas. If you don't want to make that much pizza, you can easily halve the ingredients or quarter them. You can also make the dough, prepare it up to the final stage, and then freeze the balls of dough in individual plastic freezer bags. Or bake the pizza, cool it, and freeze it, then reheat it before serving. You can also make pizzas that are larger or smaller than those in this book. A 12-ounce (350-gram) ball of dough will make a pizza that's about 12 by 10 inches, which is four substantial squares. Increase or decrease the toppings to match. Don't worry if the pizza doesn't fill the pan—focus more on stretching it to the thickness that you prefer. Remember to adjust the cooking time depending on the thickness of the dough and your oven's temperature.

Gabriele doesn't discuss pizza stones, but I experimented with using mine and I like the crispy bottom crust that it provides. If you do use a pizza stone when baking, keep a very close eye on the bottom crust, which can go quickly from a lovely golden brown to overly dark.

Natalie Danford

Index of Ingredients

A

Almonds: 136
Amaretto Cookies: 159
Anchovies: 100, 114, 115, 195, 196, 218, 234
Apricots: 101
Artichokes: 192, 226, 227
Arugula: 236
Asparagus: 220, 231

B

Baccalà: 119, 136, 183, 244
Basil: 82, 247
Beans: 176, 186
Beef: 111, 165, 224
Broccoli: 160, 162, 181, 182
Broccolini: 140
Burrata: 128

C

Cabbage: 210
Caciocavallo Cheese: 162
Cardoon: 213, 224, 236, 240, 241, 247
Chestnut: 156, 170
Chicken: 237
Chickpea: 183
Chicory: 144, 153, 177, 236
Coffee: 232
Coppa di Testa: 166, 181
Cotechino Sausage: 152
Cuttlefish: 129

D

Dandelion Greens: 189, 236
Date: 214
Duck: 201

E

Eel: 189
Eggplant: 92, 96, 104, 128
Eggs: 195, 231
Endive: 127, 234, 237

F

Fava beans: 226, 240
Fennel: 206
Figs: 89, 93
Flowers: 241
Fontina: 198
Frisée: 132

G

Gorgonzola: 198
Grana Cheese: 159, 165, 206, 213, 247
Grapes: 150, 153
Green Beans: 129
Greens: 119, 127, 132, 144, 153, 166, 177, 189, 195, 204, 234, 236, 237, 241
Grouper: 118
Gruyère: 144, 208
Guanciale: 200, 204, 226

H

Hazelnuts: 141
Honey: 248

K

Kale: 186

L

Lamb: 232
Leeks: 208
Lemon: 220, 231
Licorice: 214

M

Mango: 119
Mint: 111
Mortadella: 140, 196
Mozzarella: 81, 82, 88, 92, 96, 106, 114, 145, 188, 218, 236, 240, 241, 247
Mushrooms: 137, 148, 156, 165

N

'Nduja: 141
Nutmeg: 208

O

Octopus: 98
Olives: 110, 234
Onion: 221
Oranges: 166, 201

P

Pancetta: 172, 220
Parmigiano: 92, 220
Peaches: 127
Peas: 226
Pecorino: 198, 200, 224, 240

Peppers: 101, 106, 114, 122, 224
Persimmons: 141
Pickled Vegetables: 160
Pork: 93, 101, 122, 140, 141, 145, 152, 172, 182, 196, 200, 204, 210, 220, 226
Potatoes: 81, 96, 98, 111, 127, 129, 145, 152, 176, 214, 226
Prosciutto: 93, 122
Provolone: 172
Puntarelle: 195, 241

R

Rabbit: 153
Radicchio: 206
Radishes: 156
Ragusano Cheese: 106
Ricotta: 110, 123, 141
Rosemary Ash: 96

S

Salmon: 206
Sausage: 176, 214
Shrimp: 104, 132, 148
Snow Peas: 232
Speck: 145
Spinach: 166, 204
Squab: 156
Squash: 159, 172, 189
Squash Blossoms: 110, 218
Squid: 167, 170
Stracchino Cheese: 198

T

Taleggio: 188
Tomatoes: 78, 82, 84, 92, 100, 101, 104, 107, 115, 119, 136, 137, 162, 195, 200, 224, 241, 247
Tongue: 160
Tripe: 224
Turnips: 167

V

Veal: 170

Z

Zucchini: 88, 114, 118, 123